tempted

150 very wicked desserts

tempted
150 very wicked desserts

Joanne Glynn

Photography by Brett Stevens
Styling by Vanessa Austin

THUNDER BAY
P·R·E·S·S

San Diego, California

Thunder Bay Press
An imprint of the Advantage Publishers Group
5880 Oberlin Drive, San Diego, CA 92121–4794
www.thunderbaybooks.com

All notations of errors or omissions should be addressed to Thunder Bay Press, Editorial Department, at the above address. All other correspondence (author inquiries, permissions) concerning the content of this book should be addressed to Murdoch Books, Pier 8/9, 23 Hickson Road, Millers Point NSW 2000, Australia.

NOTE: Those who might be at risk from the effects of salmonella poisoning (the elderly, pregnant women, young children, and those with a compromised immune system) should consult their physician before trying recipes with raw eggs.

ISBN-13: 978-1-59223-694-7
ISBN-10: 1-59223-694-4

Library of Congress Cataloging-in-Publication Data available upon request.

Printed in China

1 2 3 4 5 09 08 07 06

Design Manager: Vivien Valk
Project Manager and Editor: Janine Flew
U.S. Editor: Georgina Bitcon
Food Editor: Joanne Glynn
Design Concept: Marylouise Brammer
Art Direction and Designer: Sarah Odgers
Photographer: Brett Stevens
Stylist: Vanessa Austin
Food Preparation: Grace Campbell, Joanne Kelly, Wendy Quisumbing
Recipes: Michelle Earl, Joanne Glynn, Wendy Quisumbing, and the Murdoch Books Test Kitchen
General and Chapter Introductions: Margaret Malone
Production: Adele Troeger

The publisher and stylist would like to thank the following companies for generously lending furniture, fabric, tableware, floor coverings, paint, clothes, and wallpaper for photography: 224 Bondi Rd, Bodum, Brunschwig and Fils, Chee Soon and Fitzgerald, Cloth, Country Road, Dandi, Dinosaur Designs, Domayne Design Centre, Dulux (designer silk range), ECC Lighting, Elevate Designs, Hoglund Art Glass, Husk, Jarass, Jendi, Laminex, Love Plates for VNR Australia, Major and Tom, Maxwell and Williams, Mokum Textiles, Mud Australia, Newtown Old Wares, Osborne and Little, Pazotti, Perry and Fowles, Primo Imports, Radford Furnishings, Rosenthal—Studio Line, South Pacific Fabrics, Spence and Lyda, Studio Imports, The Source Products, Tomkin Australia, Tres Fabu.

contents

the sweet life People have taken delight and pride in creating wonderful desserts for centuries, knowing that few sights make their guests' eyes light up as much as that of a delicious dessert.

Whether rich and decadent or simple and quick to prepare, all good desserts have a common theme—the enjoyment in the eating is more than matched by the pleasure had in their making.

the sweet life

It's a secret shared by all cooks that cooking a dessert is no chore. People who don't cook **marvel** at a homemade chocolate cake or a pile of still-warm brownies, convinced that the skills needed to produce such wonders are far beyond them. This is a shame, because those who do cook know it's fun, it's generally easy, and what's more, it's hugely **rewarding**. This can be true of all cooking, but it often isn't—time pressures and the necessity of producing a tasty, nutritious meal for the family night after night can mean that everyday cooking is just that—everyday. So, when the decision is made to prepare a **delicious** dessert, it's not only the recipients that are very pleased with the turn of events. The cook is, too.

Often, it takes only the gentlest nudge for the dessert chef within to awaken. It might be the purchase of a bag of **fresh** plums, or simply the change of season that turns your thoughts to loved ones and what would be **pleasing** to their tummies. But whatever the reason, the pleasure of cooking desserts begins with making that decision. After that, at every stage, it's the same: anticipation and enjoyment. Turning the pages of a cookbook, choosing the recipe, doing the planning and shopping; then onto the cooking and decorating, the serving—and of course, the eating. This may sound unlikely to those unfamiliar with the delight felt upon successfully making a lemon pie from scratch or a perfect fig and raspberry cake. But what they fail to consider is that shopping for dessert wine or good-quality mascarpone cheese is not the same as buying chops, and piping chocolate frosting is not the same as mashing potatoes. We enjoy it.

That is the guiding principle behind this book. Most of us don't make a dessert every day, or even every other day, so when we do, we want it to be wonderful—not just the result but the cooking, too. Thus the recipes here aren't out to shock but to satisfy. There is nothing tricky just for the sake of it. Presentation is important, but that needn't imply fussiness. Equally, some recipes do involve a number of steps but none require days and nights in the kitchen, rare and unusual ingredients, or obscure pieces of equipment. What creaming and beating, mixing and baking there is falls within the bounds of healthy effort. Ingredients, too, are almost entirely familiar. It's a constant wonder of chemistry how flour, eggs, sugar, butter, cocoa, and cream can produce, time and again, a new and equally irresistible creation with just a few changes of technique and variations in supporting ingredients. With the welcome presence of fruit and nuts, or the felicitous addition of alcohol, the basic building blocks of desserts start to look impressive indeed.

Without further ado, then, let us turn to the recipes themselves. This collection features a little bit of everything, so it's a good book to explore. The six chapters are divided by type, and the recipes range from a traditional crème caramel or classic brandy-laced tiramisu to light and pretty toffee-glazed poached peaches and never-fail winners such as baked chocolate desserts with rich chocolate sauce. You can be guided in your decision-making by a particular ingredient (the last of the Cointreau in the bottle), an occasion (your turn to host the monthly book club meeting), the season (cherries have arrived!), or plain old whim (you just want to cook something sweet).

Is it too much to say there is a touch of romance in making a dessert? The creativity involved in the planning and cooking, the act of giving, the exploration of an unfamiliar or foreign recipe; these all lift us out of our everyday routines for a moment. Making Italian chocolate-filled ravioli or baked apples with Pedro Ximénez sauce—Spain's legendary sherry—does indeed conjure a little bit of Italian good living or Andalusian sunshine. Such desserts let you travel the world for a delicious brief while. This is true of a lot of good cooking, of course, but whereas with a lamb chop you're traveling economy, with a rich gâteau or sumptuous soufflé, you're going first-class. If only more of life was like this, really.

Tempted is all about enjoyment and letting your imagination lead the way—regardless of whether the chosen dish is a simple sundae or an elaborate, layered frozen dessert. Once the dessert is ready, choose some nice plates, get out the good napkins, and bring out the dessert forks; it's all part of the pleasure. And what's more, everyone will love it and you for your efforts.

chocolate heaven If these rich, dark, decadent recipes are anything to go by, chocolate heaven is a land permanently locked in winter's embrace. In this wondrously hedonistic place, the

elements conspire to keep you contentedly indoors, snuggling on the sofa and warming yourself from the inside out with a luscious helping of one of these chocolate-laden desserts.

When it comes to warding off the wintry blues, few things have the restorative powers of an indulgent slice of something heavily dependent on chocolate. Smooth and creamy, heady in its sweet richness, chocolate is the ultimate dessert maker. Even the names of the cakes, desserts, tortes, and bars in this chapter send a happy tingling through the body—wicked walnut and chocolate plum torte, rich chocolate and whisky mud cake, and three chocolates pie. There is a grand, almost hedonistic tone to these recipes that brooks no resistance—chocolate filling, chocolate topping, and a bit more chocolate lovingly coating the sides. It is chocolate's wonderful versatility that makes it such a magical and pleasurable ingredient to work with in the kitchen, be it dark, milk, or white, chopped and melted, blended and baked, gloopily liquid, or in chunky bits. And when the remaining assembled ingredients include cream, sugar, eggs, nuts, liqueurs and cognacs, cinnamon, and the odd marshmallow, you know that these are recipes prepared to jump in at the deep end. It is no wonder that few chefs complain about being trapped in the kitchen when it comes to chocolate creations. So, for those of us without a crackling wood fire, cozy wood-paneled room, or faithful dog resting by our feet to defend us against the rigors of winter (or any season, really), we need not pack for sunnier shores. Instead, just turn these pages and discover how many decadent, chocolate-coated ways there are to have a little bit of heaven deliciously close by.

chocolate pots with hazelnut toffee

1²/₃ cups good-quality dark
    chocolate
2¹/₃ cups whipping cream
6 large egg yolks
¹/₃ cup superfine sugar
1 tablespoon espresso coffee,
    freshly brewed

2 tablespoons Frangelico or
    other hazelnut liqueur
²/₃ cup whole hazelnuts,
    toasted and skinned (see
    note, page 41)
1 cup superfine sugar, extra

Preheat the oven to 300°F. Finely chop the chocolate and put it in a heatproof bowl.

Gently heat the cream in a small saucepan over medium heat. Bring it just to a simmer (don't allow it to boil), then quickly remove it from the heat and pour it over the chocolate. Stir constantly until the chocolate completely melts—this will take about 5 minutes. The mixture should be smooth and have an even color.

Whisk the egg yolks with the sugar just to combine, then gradually stir in the chocolate mixture, then the coffee and liqueur. Strain the mixture through a fine sieve. Allow to settle and cool slightly, then skim off any foam on the surface.

Divide the mixture among eight ¹/₂-cup ramekins, filling to just below the top. If any air bubbles are on the surface, gently prick them with a fine skewer or tap the ramekin lightly on the counter.

Cover each ramekin tightly with foil. Put the ramekins into a large baking pan, ensuring they are evenly spaced and not too close to the edge of the pan. Pour in enough hot water to reach about halfway up the sides of the ramekins. Cook for 1 hour, then check them by gently shaking a ramekin—the mixture should be set around the edges but still wobble a little in the middle.

For the toffee, spread the hazelnuts on a lightly buttered cookie sheet. Put the sugar and 1 cup water in a small pan over high heat and stir until the sugar dissolves. Bring to a boil, then reduce the heat and simmer for 8 minutes or until the toffee turns a deep amber. Swirl the pan occasionally so that it cooks evenly, and watch carefully so that it doesn't become too dark. Take from the heat immediately and pour the toffee over the hazelnuts on the cookie sheet. Put aside and allow to set. When cool, break into uneven pieces.

Take the ramekins out of the pan, remove the foil, and allow them to cool completely before covering and refrigerating for at least 3 hours or until well chilled. Serve the chocolate pots accompanied by the hazelnut toffee.

Serves 8

chocolate roulade with black cherry kirsch cream

3 eggs
1/2 cup superfine sugar
2 teaspoons instant coffee
  granules
1/2 cup self-rising flour
1/4 cup unsweetened cocoa
  powder
1/4 cup dark chocolate, grated

1 tablespoon superfine sugar,
  extra
3/4 cup whipping cream

1 tablespoon confectioners'
  sugar
15-ounce can pitted black
  cherries, drained and halved
1/2 cup cherry jam
2 tablespoons kirsch

confectioners' sugar, to dust
  (optional)
unsweetened cocoa powder,
  to dust (optional)

Preheat the oven to 350°F. Grease a 10 x 12-inch jelly roll pan and line with parchment paper. Using electric beaters, beat the eggs in a medium bowl for 2 minutes, until pale and thick. Gradually add the sugar in a slow steady stream. Continue to beat for another 3 minutes, until the mixture is thick and creamy.

Dissolve the coffee in 1 tablespoon boiling water. Sift together the flour and cocoa powder. Using a large metal spoon, fold the sifted flour and cocoa, the chocolate, and dissolved coffee into the egg white mixture.

Mix quickly and lightly. Spread evenly into the prepared pan and smooth the surface. Bake for 12 minutes or until springy to the touch.

Put a sheet of parchment paper on a clean dish towel. Sprinkle the parchment paper with the extra superfine sugar. Turn the cake out onto the paper and carefully remove the parchment paper used for lining the pan. Let stand for 2 minutes, then roll the cake and parchment paper from one short end and set aside for 5 minutes or until cool.

Meanwhile, beat the cream and confectioners' sugar until thick, then fold through the cherries. Combine the jam and kirsch in a small bowl. Carefully unroll the cake. Trim the long edges with a sharp knife to neaten. Evenly spread with the jam and kirsch. Spread the cream and cherries over the cake, leaving a 2-inch edge on the back short side. Roll up with the aid of the parchment paper, enclosing the cream and cherries.

Sprinkle liberally with the cocoa powder and confectioners' sugar. With the seam underneath, carefully lift the roulade onto a serving plate. Serve immediately or cover with plastic wrap and refrigerate for up to 1 hour. Cut into thick slices to serve.

Serves 8–10

chocolate roulade with black cherry
kirsch cream

creamy chocolate mousse

1 cup dark chocolate, chopped
4 eggs, separated
3/4 cup whipping cream

extra whipped cream, to serve
unsweetened cocoa powder,
    to serve

Melt the chocolate in a heatproof bowl set over a saucepan of simmering water, making sure the bottom of the bowl does not touch the water. Stir until smooth, then remove from the heat to cool slightly. Lightly beat the egg yolks and stir them into the chocolate. Lightly whip the cream and gently fold it into the chocolate mixture until it is velvety.

Beat the egg whites to soft peaks. Using a metal spoon, fold one spoonful of the egg white into the mousse to lighten it, then gently fold in the remainder—the secret is to use a light, quick touch.

You only need small quantities of the mousse—spoon it into six small wine glasses or 3/4-cup ramekins. Cover with plastic wrap and refrigerate until set, about 4 hours or overnight. When ready to serve, add some whipped cream and a dusting of cocoa powder.

Serves 6

chocolate rum fondue

1²/₃ cups dark chocolate, chopped

¹/₂ cup whipping cream

1–2 tablespoons rum

1 mandarin, tangerine, or small orange, peeled and divided into segments

12 cherries with stalks

2 fresh figs, quartered lengthwise

1²/₃ cups strawberries, hulled

2³/₄ cups white marshmallows

Melt the chocolate and cream in a medium heatproof bowl over a saucepan of simmering water, making sure the bottom of the bowl doesn't touch the water. Stir until smooth, remove from the heat, and stir in the rum to taste. While warm, pour into the fondue pot.

Arrange the fruit and marshmallows on a serving platter and serve to dip into the chocolate fondue.

Note: Use a selection of whatever fruit is in season, and if they need to be cut, choose those that don't have a moist surface.

Serves 6

chocolate swirl pavlova with dipped strawberries

1/2 cup dark chocolate, chopped
2 1/2 cups medium strawberries
4 egg whites
pinch cream of tartar
1 1/4 cups superfine sugar
1 cup whipping cream
1 tablespoon strawberry
  or raspberry liqueur

1 tablespoon confectioners'
  sugar
3 tablespoons strawberry jam
1 tablespoon strawberry or
  raspberry liqueur, extra

Melt the chocolate in a small bowl over a saucepan of simmering water, making sure that the bottom of the bowl does not touch the water. Dip 8 of the strawberries partially into the chocolate, then put them on a sheet of parchment paper and leave to set. Reserve the remaining melted chocolate. Hull the remaining strawberries. Cut some in half lengthwise, leaving the rest whole. Refrigerate until needed.

Preheat the oven to 300°F. Grease a cookie sheet or pizza pan and line with parchment paper. Using electric beaters, whisk the egg whites until firm peaks form. Add the cream of tartar, then the sugar in a slow steady stream, beating continuously. Then continue to beat until the meringue is glossy and very thick, about 5 minutes.

Spoon one-third of the meringue onto the prepared sheet and spread it into a rough 9-inch circle. With a spoon, drizzle over one-third of the reserved melted chocolate, making swirls of chocolate in a marbled effect. Top with more meringue and chocolate drizzle, then repeat once more. Use a metal spatula to flatten slightly and smooth the surface.

Bake until the edges and top are dry, about 50 minutes. Turn off the heat, leave the oven door slightly ajar, and allow the meringue to cool fully.

Beat the cream, liqueur, and confectioners' sugar until thick. To serve, turn out the pavlova onto a wire rack, peel off the parchment paper, and invert it onto a serving platter. Spread with the whipped cream. Arrange the whole and halved strawberries all over the top of the cream, interspersing them with the chocolate-coated strawberries.

Warm the strawberry jam, then sieve it and stir in the liqueur. Use a pastry brush to coat the strawberries in a random fashion, until they look glossy. Cut into thick wedges and serve at once.

Serves 8–10

chocolate swirl pavlova
with dipped strawberries

double chocolate brownies

1/3 cup butter	2 eggs, lightly beaten
1/3 cup unsweetened cocoa powder	1/2 cup all-purpose flour
	1/2 teaspoon baking powder
2/3 cup superfine sugar	1/2 cup chocolate chips

Preheat the oven to 350°F. Grease an 8-inch square cake pan and line with parchment paper.

Melt the butter in a medium saucepan, then remove from the heat and stir in the cocoa and sugar, followed by the eggs. Sift the flour, baking powder, and a pinch of salt into the saucepan, then mix it in. Make sure you don't have any pockets of flour. Stir in the chocolate chips.

Pour the mixture into the prepared pan and bake for 30 minutes. The brownies are cooked when a skewer or knife poked into the middle comes out clean or with just a few dryish crumbs attached. (Remember that the chocolate chips may have melted and it might look as if the mixture is still wet if your skewer hits one of those.) Let the brownies cool in the pan, then turn out and cut into squares.

Makes 12

chocolate croissant pudding

4 croissants, torn into pieces
1 cup dark chocolate, chopped
4 eggs
heaping ¼ cup superfine sugar
1 cup milk
1 cup whipping cream
3 teaspoons orange liqueur

3 teaspoons grated orange zest
4 tablespoons orange juice
2 tablespoons hazelnuts,
 roughly chopped
heavy cream, to serve

Preheat the oven to 350°F. Grease an 8-inch round deep-sided cake pan and line the bottom with parchment paper. Put the croissant pieces and 2/3 cup of the chopped chocolate into the pan.

Beat the eggs and sugar together until pale and creamy. Heat the milk, cream, liqueur, and remaining chocolate in a saucepan until almost boiling. Stir to melt the chocolate, then remove the pan from the heat. Gradually add to the egg mixture, stirring constantly. Stir in the orange zest and juice. Pour the mixture over the croissants, a little at a time, allowing the liquid to be fully absorbed before adding more. Sprinkle the hazelnuts over the top and bake for 50 minutes or until a skewer inserted into the center comes out clean. Cool for 10 minutes. Turn the pudding out and invert onto a serving plate. Slice and serve warm with cream.

Serves 6–8

The slight bitterness of dark chocolate counteracts the richness of these delicious and very grown-up desserts.

dark chocolate desserts with rich coffee liqueur mocha sauce

1/2 cup butter, softened
1/2 cup superfine sugar
1 teaspoon pure vanilla extract
2 eggs
1 cup all-purpose flour
1/2 cup unsweetened cocoa
    powder
2 teaspoons baking powder
scant 1/2 cup milk
1/2 cup dark chocolate, finely
    chopped

coffee liqueur mocha sauce
2 tablespoons butter
2/3 cup dark chocolate, chopped
2/3 cup whipping cream
1 teaspoon instant coffee
    powder
2 tablespoons coffee-flavored
    liqueur (such as crème de
    cacao or Kahlùa)

1/4 cup roasted hazelnuts,
    skinned and chopped (see
    note, page 41)
whipping cream, to serve
    (optional)
fresh berries, to serve (optional)

Preheat the oven to 350°F. Grease six 1-cup metal molds and put them on a cookie sheet. In a medium bowl, beat the butter, sugar, and vanilla with electric beaters for 2 minutes until thick and creamy. Add the eggs one at a time, beating well after each addition. Fold in the combined sifted flour, cocoa, and baking powder with a metal spoon, adding the milk alternately with the flour mixture. Stir in the chocolate. Spoon the mixture into the molds and smooth the surface. Bake until risen and just firm to the touch, about 15 minutes. Leave for 5 minutes, then run a small flat-bladed knife between the desserts and the molds and turn them out onto a wire rack.

Meanwhile, for the sauce, combine the butter, chocolate, cream, and coffee powder in a small saucepan over low heat. Stir until the chocolate melts and the mixture is smooth. Remove from the heat and stir in the liqueur. Keep the mixture warm. To serve, put the hot desserts on serving plates, pour over some of the sauce, sprinkle with a few chopped hazelnuts, and serve with whipping cream and berries if desired.

Note: The desserts and sauce can be reheated in a microwave oven just before serving.

Serves 6

dark chocolate desserts with rich
coffee liqueur mocha sauce

Chocolate and nuts seem made for each other; adding brandy
and mascarpone simply serves to turn delicious into irresistible.

chocolate and almond torte

1³/4 cups sliced almonds
   (or 1 cup whole almonds)
1 slice pandoro (see note) or
   1 individual brioche
2 cups dark chocolate, chopped
2 tablespoons brandy
³/4 cup unsalted butter, softened

²/3 cup superfine sugar
4 eggs
1 teaspoon pure vanilla extract
scant 1 cup mascarpone cheese
unsweetened cocoa powder,
   to dust
crème fraîche, to serve

Preheat the oven to 325°F. Put the almonds on a cookie sheet and toast
in the oven for 8–10 minutes until golden brown. Allow to cool, then put
the almonds and pandoro in a food processor and process until the
mixture resembles bread crumbs.

Lightly grease a 9-inch round springform cake pan. Pour some of the nut
mixture into the pan and shake it around so that it forms a coating on the
bottom and sides of the pan. Set the remaining nut mixture aside.

Stirring occasionally, gently melt the chocolate and brandy in a heatproof bowl set over a saucepan of simmering water, making sure the bottom of the bowl doesn't touch the water. Allow to cool slightly.

Cream the butter and sugar in a food processor or with a wooden spoon for a few minutes until light and pale. Add the melted chocolate, eggs, vanilla, and mascarpone. Add the remaining nut mixture and mix well. Pour into the pan. Bake for 50–60 minutes or until just set. Leave in the pan for 15 minutes before removing from the mold. Dust with a little cocoa when cool, and serve with crème fraîche.

Note: Pandoro is a type of light, sweet Italian yeast bread.

Serves 8–10

chocolate praline crêpes

filling

1/3 cup milk chocolate, chopped

1/3 cup dark chocolate, chopped

1/3 cup almond praline, croccante, or Vienna almonds

7 tablespoons unsalted butter, softened

2 tablespoons confectioners' sugar

1 tablespoon cognac or brandy

crêpes

1 cup all-purpose flour

1 tablespoon confectioners' sugar

2 eggs

1 1/4 cups milk

1 tablespoon cognac or brandy

2 tablespoons butter, melted

unsalted butter, for frying

2 tablespoons cognac or brandy, to serve

heavy cream, to serve

For the filling, melt both chocolates together in a small heatproof bowl set over a saucepan of simmering water by stirring frequently and making sure the bottom of the bowl doesn't touch the water. Allow to cool. In a small food processor or using a sharp knife, chop the almond praline. Don't pulverize it; leave it with some texture. Stir it through the chocolate mixture.

Beat the butter and confectioners' sugar with electric beaters until light and fluffy. Stir in the cognac and melted chocolate. Cover and refrigerate until solid.

For the crêpes, sift the flour, confectioners' sugar, and a pinch of salt into a bowl. Lightly beat the eggs, milk, cognac, and butter in a pouring bowl, then pour it into the flour mixture. Beat until you have a smooth, light batter. Cover and set aside to rest for 30 minutes or so.

Melt a little butter in an 8-inch crêpe pan over medium–low heat. Pour in a small ladleful of batter (2–3 tablespoons), and quickly swirl the pan so that the batter spreads evenly over the bottom. You want the crêpes as thin as possible. Cook until bubbles start to appear in the center and the edges become crisp. Flip the crêpe over and brown the other side. Transfer to a plate and repeat with the rest of the batter. You will need 8 crêpes, and there is enough mixture for a trial run.

Preheat a broiler to high. Put some chocolate filling down the center of each crêpe and roll them up. Arrange the filled crêpes in a shallow heatproof dish. Put under the broiler until the chocolate filling melts (15 50 seconds), then remove. Immediately sprinkle the cognac over the top and carefully put a flame to it. The cognac will ignite and burn off the alcohol. Serve at once with heavy cream.

Serves 8

chocolate praline crêpes

chocolate hazelnut cake

1¹/2 cups hazelnuts, roasted and skinned (see note)
1¹/3 cups dark chocolate, chopped
2 teaspoons instant coffee granules
³/4 cup cornstarch
heaping ³/4 cup unsalted butter, softened

³/4 cup superfine sugar
4 eggs, separated
2 teaspoons hazelnut or coffee liqueur
confectioners' sugar, to serve
chocolate curls, to serve (see page 61) (optional)
crème fraîche or vanilla ice cream, to serve

Preheat the oven to 325°F. Grease an 8-inch round springform cake pan.

Put the hazelnuts and chocolate in a small processor fitted with a metal blade and process in 5-second bursts until finely chopped. Add the coffee granules and cornstarch and process briefly to combine. Transfer to a small bowl and set aside.

Change the blade on the processor to the plastic blade. Add the butter and sugar and process in 3-second bursts until pale. Add one-quarter of the chocolate mixture and process in short bursts to combine, then add 1 egg yolk and mix through in short bursts. Continue in this way until all the chocolate mixture and egg yolks have been added. Add the liqueur and process in short bursts to combine. Transfer to a bowl.

Whisk the egg whites until soft peaks form. Using a metal spoon, fold a large scoop of egg white into the chocolate mixture. Gently fold in the remaining egg white. Spoon into the prepared pan, level the surface, and bake for 30 minutes. Cover loosely with foil and bake for 30–35 minutes more or until a skewer inserted in the center of the cake comes out clean. The surface of the cake will probably crack.

Serve the cake warm or at room temperature. Dust the surface with confectioners' sugar and sprinkle with chocolate curls, if using. Cut the cake into slices; the texture will be quite moist. Serve with a scoop of crème fraîche or softened vanilla ice cream.

Note: To roast and skin hazelnuts, spread in a single layer in a roasting pan and toast in a moderate oven for 10 minutes or so, stirring occasionally until fragrant and golden. Tip the hot nuts into a clean dish towel, gather up the corners, and rub to remove most of the skins. Not all of the skins will come off; don't worry about those that don't.

Serves 6–8

wicked walnut and chocolate plum torte

2 cups walnuts
1 1/3 cups dark chocolate, chilled
and chopped
2 teaspoons instant coffee
granules
heaping 3/4 cup cornstarch
1 cup butter, softened
3/4 cup superfine sugar

4 eggs, separated
2 teaspoons coffee liqueur
2 tablespoons dark brown sugar
1 pound small firm plums or
12 ounces medium to large
plums, halved and pitted
vanilla ice cream or whipped
cream, to serve

Preheat the oven to 325°F. Grease a 10-inch round springform cake pan and line the bottom with parchment paper.

Grind the walnuts and chocolate together in a food processor until finely processed. Add the coffee granules and cornstarch and process briefly to combine.

Reserve 1 tablespoon butter. In a large bowl, cream the remaining butter and the superfine sugar with electric beaters until pale. Add the egg yolks, one at a time, alternately with some of the walnut mixture, beating well after each addition. Stir in the liqueur.

Whisk the egg whites until soft peaks form. Fold a large spoonful into the walnut mixture, then gently fold the rest of the egg white through. Spoon into the prepared pan and level the surface. Bake for 30 minutes.

Remove the cake from the oven and arrange the plums on top of the cake, cut side up. Sprinkle with the brown sugar and dot the remaining 1 tablespoon butter over the sugar. Return to the oven. Bake until a skewer inserted in the center comes out clean, about 40 minutes longer.

Remove from the oven and allow to cool for 1 minute, then carefully run a knife around the edge to prevent the melted brown sugar from sticking to the pan. Cool in the pan for 15 minutes before turning out onto a wire rack. Serve warm in slices, accompanied by softened vanilla ice cream or whipped vanilla cream.

Serves 8–10

wicked walnut and chocolate
plum torte

Sweetened, dried cranberries (sometimes sold as Craisins) add a slight chewiness to this nut-flavored meringue gâteau.

white chocolate, almond, and cranberry torte

8 egg whites
1 cup superfine sugar
2 cups good-quality white
  chocolate, chopped
1¼ cups whole blanched
  almonds, toasted and
  chopped

1½ cups sweetened dried
  cranberries
⅓ cup self-rising flour

Preheat the oven to 350°F. Grease a 9½-inch round springform cake pan and line the bottom with parchment paper. Dust the inside of the pan with a little flour, shaking out any excess.

Using electric beaters, whisk the egg whites in a clean, dry bowl until stiff peaks form. Gradually add the sugar, whisking well after each addition. Whisk until the mixture is stiff and glossy and all the sugar has dissolved.

Put the chocolate, almonds, and cranberries into a bowl, add the flour, and toss to combine. Gently fold the chocolate mixture into the egg whites. Spread the mixture into the prepared pan and gently tap the bottom on a work surface.

Bake for 1 hour, covering the cake with foil halfway through cooking if it begins to brown too quickly. Turn off the oven and leave the cake to cool completely in the oven. Run a knife around the edge of the pan to loosen the torte, then remove it from the pan.

The torte will keep, stored in an airtight container in a cool place, for up to 1 week. It is not suitable to freeze.

Serves 8–10

chocolate malakoff

1/3 cup coffee liqueur
9 ounces (20 large or 30 small) Italian ladyfingers (savoiardi)
1/2 cup dark chocolate, chopped
1/2 cup unsalted butter, softened
2/3 cup superfine sugar
1/2 teaspoon pure vanilla extract
1 1/4 cups almonds, ground

1/2 cup whipping cream, whipped
1 1/4 cups fresh or thawed frozen raspberries, plus extra fresh raspberries to serve (optional)
unsweetened cocoa powder, to dust
confectioners' sugar, to dust

Line a deep 6-cup bowl with plastic wrap, allowing enough to hang over to use as handles when removing the dessert from the mold. Mix half the liqueur with 1 tablespoon water in a small bowl. Dip the smooth sides of the ladyfingers briefly into the liquid and use them to neatly line the bottom and sides of the bowl, smooth sides inward. Stand them upright around the sides and trim them to fit snugly.

Stirring frequently, melt the chocolate in a small heatproof bowl set over a saucepan of gently simmering water, making sure that the bottom of the bowl does not touch the water. Remove the bowl from the heat and stir in the remaining coffee liqueur, including any liquid left over from dipping the biscuits.

Cream the butter and sugar with electric beaters until pale and fluffy. Fold through the melted chocolate. Add the vanilla and almonds and fold in lightly but thoroughly. Fold in the whipped cream.

Spoon one-quarter of the mixture into the bowl. Cover with one-third of the raspberries, then repeat the layering twice. Finish with the remaining one-quarter of the mixture smoothed over the top. If you have any ladyfingers left, they can go on top if you like, but this isn't essential. Cover and refrigerate overnight to set.

Use the plastic wrap to lever the dessert out of the bowl (you can also run a knife around the inside of the bowl to help loosen it), then invert it onto a serving plate. Remove the plastic wrap. Dust the top with cocoa, letting some of it drift down the sides. Lightly dust confectioners' sugar on top of the cocoa. Cut into slices and serve with extra raspberries if desired.

Serves 6–8

chocolate malakoff

white chocolate torte

3 eggs, at room temperature
1/3 cup superfine sugar
1/2 cup white chocolate,
    chopped and melted
1/2 cup all-purpose flour, sifted
white chocolate curls, to serve
    (see page 61)

topping
scant 2/3 cup whipping cream
1 2/3 cups white chocolate,
    chopped
1/2 cup mascarpone cheese

Preheat the oven to 350°F. Grease an 8-inch round springform cake pan. Beat the eggs and sugar with an electric beater until thick and pale. Fold in the melted white chocolate and sifted flour. Pour into the prepared pan and bake for 20 minutes or until a skewer inserted into the center of the cake comes out clean. Leave in the pan to cool.

For the topping, put the cream and white chocolate in a saucepan. Stir constantly over low heat for 5–6 minutes or until the chocolate melts and the mixture is smooth. Remove from the heat and set aside to cool slightly. Stir the mascarpone into the chocolate mixture. Remove the cake from the pan and use a spatula to spread the topping over the top and sides. Refrigerate overnight or until the topping is firm. Serve sprinkled with the chocolate curls.

Serves 6–8

white chocolate and raspberry ripple rice pudding

1 cup fresh raspberries
2 tablespoons confectioners'
    sugar
2 tablespoons raspberry liqueur,
    such as Framboise
2 tablespoons unsalted butter
heaping 1/2 cup risotto rice

1 vanilla bean, split
31/4 cups milk
1/4 cup superfine sugar
1 teaspoon pure vanilla extract
2/3 cup white chocolate,
    chopped

Using a hand blender, purée the berries, confectioners' sugar, and liqueur.

Melt the butter in a large nonstick saucepan. Add the rice and vanilla bean and stir until the rice is coated in the butter. Heat the milk, superfine sugar, and vanilla extract to just below boiling point. Ladle a spoonful of the milk mixture into the rice and stir constantly until the liquid has been absorbed. Repeat until all the milk mixture has been added and the rice is tender. Remove the vanilla bean. (It can be dried and later reused).

Add the white chocolate and stir until melted. Set aside for 5 minutes, then spoon the rice pudding into bowls. Swirl the raspberry purée through the rice to create a ripple effect.

Serves 4

rich chocolate and whisky mud cake with crystallized violets

1 cup butter, chopped
1 1/3 cups dark chocolate, chopped
1 2/3 cup superfine sugar
1/2 cup whisky
1 tablespoon instant coffee granules
1 1/2 cups all-purpose flour
1/2 cup self-rising flour
1/3 cup unsweetened cocoa powder
2 eggs, lightly beaten
3 tablespoons whisky, extra

chocolate glaze
1/3 cup whipping cream
2/3 cup dark chocolate, chopped

crystallized violets, to decorate (optional; see note)
silver dragées, to decorate (optional)

Preheat the oven to 315°F. Grease an 8-inch square cake pan and line the bottom and sides with parchment paper.

Put the butter, chocolate, sugar, and whisky in a medium saucepan. Dissolve the coffee granules in 1/2 cup hot water and add to the mixture. Stir over low heat until melted and smooth.

Sift the all-purpose flour, self-rising flour, and cocoa into a large bowl. Pour the butter mixture into the flour mixture and whisk until just combined. Whisk in the eggs. Pour into the prepared pan.

Bake until a skewer comes out clean when inserted in the center of the cake, about 1 hour and 15 minutes. Pour the extra whisky over the hot cooked cake. Leave in the pan for 20 minutes, then turn out onto a wire rack placed over a cookie sheet to cool completely.

For the chocolate glaze, put the cream in a small saucepan and bring just to a boil. Remove from the heat and add the chocolate. Stir until combined and smooth. Set aside to cool and thicken a little. Spread the glaze over the cake, allowing it to drizzle over the sides. Leave to set. Decorate with the crystallized violets and silver dragées.

Note: To make the crystallized violets, use a small, clean artist's paintbrush to coat 16 fresh organic violets with a thin layer of lightly beaten egg white. Sprinkle evenly with superfine sugar. Set the violets on a wire rack and leave to dry. When dry, store in an airtight container between layers of tissue. The violets are edible.

Serves 16

rich chocolate and whisky mud cake
with crystallized violets

Dense, chewy brownies are delicious just as they are, or pile them high and add candles for a birthday cake with a difference.

cashew brownies

1 1/3 cups dark chocolate, chopped

3/4 cup unsalted butter, chopped

2 eggs

1 cup dark brown sugar, firmly packed

1/3 cup unsweetened cocoa powder

1 cup all-purpose flour

1/2 cup unsalted cashews, toasted and chopped

2/3 cup dark chocolate, chopped, extra

frosting

1 1/3 cups dark chocolate, chopped

1/2 cup sour cream

1/4 cup confectioners' sugar, sifted

Preheat the oven to 315°F. Grease a 9-inch square cake pan and line the bottom with parchment paper.

Stirring frequently, melt the chocolate and butter in a heatproof bowl set over a saucepan of gently simmering water, making sure the base of the bowl does not touch the water. Allow to cool.

Whisk the eggs and sugar in a large bowl for 5 minutes or until pale and thick. Fold in the cooled chocolate mixture, then the sifted cocoa powder and flour. Fold in the cashews and extra chocolate, then pour into the pan, smoothing the top. Bake for 30–35 minutes or until just firm to the touch. (The brownies may have a slightly soft center when hot but will become firm when cool.) Allow to cool.

For the frosting, melt and stir the chocolate in a small heatproof bowl set over a saucepan of gently simmering water. Cool slightly, then add the sour cream and confectioners' sugar and mix well. Spread evenly over the cooled brownies. Leave for a few hours or overnight, then cut into squares. The brownies will keep, stored in an airtight container, for up to 5 days. Unfrosted brownies may be stored for up to 3 months in the freezer. Thaw fully before frosting.

Makes 25

devil's food cake with strawberry cream

2¼ cups self-rising flour
⅔ cup unsweetened cocoa
    powder
1 teaspoon baking soda
1½ cups superfine sugar
3 eggs, lightly beaten
⅔ cup butter, softened

chocolate curls
⅔ cup milk chocolate, chopped
⅔ cup white chocolate,
    chopped

ganache
1½ cups dark chocolate,
    chopped
5 tablespoons butter

strawberry cream
1 cup whipping cream
2 tablespoons confectioners'
    sugar
1 teaspoon pure vanilla extract
1¾ cups strawberries
4 tablespoons strawberry jam
2 tablespoons orange liqueur,
    such as Grand Marnier or
    Cointreau
confectioners' sugar

Preheat the oven to 350°F. Grease a 9½-inch round cake pan and line the bottom with parchment paper. Sift the flour, cocoa, and baking soda into a large bowl. Add the sugar, eggs, butter, and 1 cup water. Using electric beaters, beat on low speed for 1 minute. Increase the speed to high and beat for another 4 minutes. Pour into the prepared pan.

Bake until a skewer inserted into the center of the cake comes out clean, about 55 minutes. Leave in the pan for 20 minutes before turning onto a wire rack to cool completely.

For the chocolate curls, melt both chocolates separately in small heatproof bowls over saucepans of gently simmering water, making sure the bowls do not touch the water. Spread separately in thin layers onto a flat surface. Leave until set. Using a knife at a 45-degree angle, form long thin curls by pushing the knife through the chocolate away from you. Refrigerate until needed. For the ganache, melt the chocolate and butter in a heatproof bowl over a saucepan of gently simmering water. Set aside to cool slightly.

For the strawberry cream, beat the cream and confectioners' sugar together until thick using electric beaters. Refrigerate until needed. Set aside 8 whole strawberries; hull and chop the remainder. Just before using, fold the chopped strawberries and vanilla through the cream. Combine the jam and liqueur in a small bowl. Cut the cake in half horizontally. Place the bottom half on a serving plate and spread evenly with the jam, then the strawberry cream. Top with the other cake half. Spread the ganache smoothly over the top of the cake. Arrange the milk chocolate and white chocolate curls and the strawberries decoratively over the cake. Dust all over with confectioners' sugar just prior to serving. Cut the cake into wedges and serve.

Serves 8–10

devil's food cake with
strawberry cream

flourless chocolate cake

1 cup dark chocolate, chopped
1/2 cup unsalted butter, chopped
2/3 cup superfine sugar
5 eggs, separated
1 3/4 cups ground hazelnuts
1/2 teaspoon baking powder
1/3 cup unsweetened cocoa
    powder
1 teaspoon ground cinnamon
confectioners' sugar, to dust

vanilla cream
1 vanilla bean or 1 teaspoon
    pure vanilla extract
1/2 pint whipping cream
1 tablespoon superfine sugar

Preheat the oven to 325°F. Lightly grease an 8-inch round cake pan and line the bottom with parchment paper.

Stirring frequently, melt the chocolate in a heatproof bowl set over a saucepan of gently simmering water, making sure the bottom of the bowl does not touch the water. Set aside and allow to cool.

Using electric beaters, cream the butter and sugar in a large bowl until pale and fluffy. Add the egg yolks one at a time, beating well after each addition. Fold in the cooled, melted chocolate.

Sift the hazelnuts, baking powder, cocoa powder, and cinnamon into a bowl, then fold into the butter mixture.

Whisk the egg whites in a clean, dry bowl until stiff peaks form. Using a large metal spoon, fold the egg whites into the chocolate mixture, working in two batches. Gently spread the mixture into the pan and bake for about 1 hour or until a skewer inserted into the center of the cake comes out clean. Allow the cake to cool in the pan.

Meanwhile, make the vanilla cream. If using the vanilla bean, split it down the middle and scrape out the seeds. Beat the cream, vanilla seeds (or extract), and sugar in a small bowl using electric beaters until soft peaks form. Serve the cake dusted with confectioners' sugar and with the vanilla cream.

This cake will keep, stored in an airtight container, for 3–4 days. It is also suitable to freeze.

Serves 6–8

white chocolate parfait with almond praline

¹/₄ cup superfine sugar

2 teaspoons instant coffee
   granules

1 cup white chocolate, chopped

3 egg yolks

3 tablespoons Marsala

1 cup whipping cream

almond praline

¹/₃ cup whole blanched
   almonds, lightly toasted and
   coarsely chopped

¹/₃ cup superfine sugar

extra Marsala, to drizzle

Put the sugar and 4 tablespoons water in a small saucepan. Stir to dissolve the sugar, then bring to a boil. Reduce the heat and simmer for 4 minutes.

Meanwhile, dissolve the coffee in 2 teaspoons of hot water. Put the chopped white chocolate in a food processor and process until fine. With the motor running, pour on the hot syrup, then add the egg yolks, coffee, and Marsala. Process until smooth. Transfer the mixture to a medium bowl.

In another bowl, beat the cream until firm. Use a metal spoon to fold the cream into the white chocolate mixture. Mix gently until smooth. Divide among six small wine glasses. Place on a tray, cover, and refrigerate for at least 3 hours.

For the praline, put the almonds on a lightly greased cookie sheet. Put the sugar and $1/4$ cup water in a small saucepan. Stir until the sugar dissolves, then increase the heat to a boil. Boil without stirring until the sugar caramelizes, 4–5 minutes. Pour over the almonds to coat. Leave to harden, then break into pieces and coarsely chop. Store in an airtight container until needed.

Before serving, place the parfaits in the freezer until very cold, about 30 minutes. To serve, decorate with some of the praline and pour a little extra Marsala onto the parfaits. Serve immediately while very cold.

Serves 6

white chocolate parfait with
almond praline

three chocolates pie

pastry

1 1/4 cups all-purpose flour

2 1/2 tablespoons unsweetened
  cocoa powder

5 tablespoons unsalted butter,
  chilled and cubed

3 tablespoons superfine sugar

4 egg yolks

1/4 teaspoon pure vanilla extract

filling

1 cup white chocolate, chopped

3 tablespoons light corn syrup

1 1/3 cups dark chocolate,
  chopped

1/2 pint whipping cream

ganache

2 tablespoons dark chocolate,
  chopped

1 tablespoon unsalted butter

1 tablespoon whipping cream

For the pastry, process the flour, cocoa, and butter in a food processor until the mixture resembles fine bread crumbs. Add the sugar and process in short bursts to mix through. Add the egg yolks, vanilla, and 1 tablespoon water. Process to form a smooth dough. Flatten to a disk, cover with plastic wrap, and chill for 45 minutes.

Preheat the oven to 350°F. Grease an 8-inch loose-bottomed fluted pie pan. Roll the pastry out thinly between two sheets of parchment paper and use to line the prepared pan, pressing it into the flutes. Cover with a sheet of parchment paper, fill with pastry weights or dried beans, and bake blind for 12 minutes. Remove the parchment paper and weights and bake until crisp and dry, about 5 minutes more. Allow to cool completely.

For the filling, put the white chocolate in a bowl set over a saucepan of simmering water, making sure that the water doesn't touch the bottom of the bowl. Heat until melted and smooth. Spoon into the piecrust and spread evenly over the bottom using the back of a spoon. Cool until set.

Put the corn syrup and dark chocolate in a small bowl over a saucepan of simmering water. Stirring often, heat until melted. It will be very thick and tacky. Transfer to a medium bowl and allow to cool.

Whip the cream to stiff peaks. Fold a heaping spoonful of cream into the chocolate mixture to loosen it. Add the rest of the cream and fold through; the mixture will become very smooth and glossy. Spoon into the piecrust, leaving it in broad swirls across the surface. Refrigerate until set.

For the ganache, put the chocolate, butter, and cream in a small bowl and set over a saucepan of simmering water. Stir until smooth and glossy. Remove from the heat and cool. Spoon the ganache into a pastry bag fitted with a 1/8-inch tip (or use a sturdy plastic bag and snip off a corner). Pipe a crisscross pattern, like an uneven grid, over the pie. Refrigerate until set before serving. Cut into slices using a hot knife.

Serves 8

chocolate mousse meringue cake

6 eggs, separated
1²/₃ cups superfine sugar
2¹/₂ tablespoons unsweetened
   cocoa powder
1¹/₃ cups dark chocolate, melted

1 tablespoon instant coffee
   granules
2 cups whipping cream,
   whipped

Preheat the oven to 300°F. Cut four pieces of parchment paper large enough to line four cookie sheets. On three of the pieces of paper, mark an 8³/₄-inch circle. On the remaining piece, draw straight lines 1¹/₄ inches apart. Line the cookie sheets with the paper.

Put the egg whites in a large, dry bowl, leave for a few minutes to warm to room temperature, then beat until soft peaks form. Gradually add the sugar, beating well after each addition. Beat for 5–10 minutes, until thick and glossy and the sugar has dissolved. Fold the sifted cocoa into the meringue.

Divide the meringue into four portions. Spread three portions over the marked circles. Put the remaining portion in a pastry bag fitted with a ¹/₂-inch plain piping tip. Pipe lines about 3¹/₂ inches long over the marked lines. Bake for 45 minutes or until pale and crisp. Check the meringue strips occasionally to prevent overcooking. Turn off the oven and cool in the oven with the door ajar.

Dissolve the coffee granules in 1 tablespoon water. Put the melted chocolate in a bowl, whisk in the egg yolks and the coffee mixture, and beat until smooth. Fold in the whipped cream and mix until combined. Refrigerate until the mousse is cold and thick.

To assemble, place one meringue disk on a plate and spread with one-third of the mousse. Top with another disk and spread with half the remaining mousse. Repeat with the remaining disk and mousse. Run a knife around the edge of the meringue cake to spread the mousse evenly over the edge. Cut or break the strips into short pieces and pile them on top of the cake, pressing them into the mousse. Dust with extra cocoa powder and refrigerate until firm.

Serves 10–12

chocolate mousse meringue cake

A chocoholic's dream—three layers of dense chocolate cake held together and topped with an indulgently rich frosting.

chocolate ganache log

cake
heaping 3/4 cup unsalted butter,
    softened
2/3 cup superfine sugar
6 eggs, at room temperature,
    separated
1 1/4 cups almonds, ground
1 cup good-quality dark
    chocolate, chopped, melted

ganache
2/3 cup whipping cream
1 1/2 cups good-quality
    bittersweet chocolate,
    chopped
2 teaspoons instant coffee
    granules

For the cake, preheat the oven to 350°F. Grease the sides of a 10 x 12-inch shallow cake pan and line the bottom with parchment paper. Beat the butter and sugar with electric beaters until light and fluffy. Add the egg yolks, one at a time, beating well after each addition. Stir in the ground almonds and melted chocolate. Beat the egg whites in a separate bowl until stiff peaks form, then gently fold into the chocolate mixture. Spread the mixture into the prepared pan and bake for 15 minutes.

Reduce the oven to 315°F and bake for another 30–35 minutes or until a skewer comes out clean when inserted into the center of the cake. Turn out the cake onto a wire rack to cool. For the ganache, put the cream and chopped chocolate in a heatproof bowl over a small saucepan of barely simmering water, making sure the bottom of the bowl doesn't touch the water. Stir occasionally until melted and combined. Stir in the coffee until it has dissolved. Set aside to cool for 2 hours or until thickened to a spreading consistency.

Cut the cake lengthwise into three even pieces. Place one piece on a serving plate and spread with a layer of ganache. Top with another layer of cake and another layer of ganache, followed by the remaining cake. Refrigerate for 30 minutes to set slightly. Cover the top and sides of the log with the remaining ganache and refrigerate for 3 hours or overnight.

Serves 8–10

Rich, creamy panna cotta becomes extra delectable with the addition of chocolate, figs, and hazelnuts.

chocolate panna cotta with figs and hazelnuts

1 cup whipping cream
1 cup milk
1 cup dark chocolate, chopped
1/4 cup superfine sugar
1/2 teaspoon pure vanilla extract
3 teaspoons powdered gelatin
6 fresh figs
2 tablespoons brown sugar

whipped cream or mascarpone
　　cheese, to serve
1/4 cup roasted hazelnuts,
　　skinned and chopped (see
　　note, page 41)

Put the cream, milk, chocolate, sugar, and vanilla in a saucepan. Stir over low heat until the mixture is smooth. Bring slowly just to a boil, then remove from the heat. Set aside.

Put the gelatin in 2 tablespoons of cold water and stir to dissolve. Add to the warm chocolate mixture and stir well. Strain the mixture into a pitcher, then pour evenly among six 1/2-cup dariole or ceramic molds. Put on a tray, cover with plastic wrap, and refrigerate until set, 4–6 hours or overnight. Even after this, it will still be quite wobbly.

To remove from the molds, briefly dip them into hot water and loosen the edges at the top by gently easing them away from the molds with your thumb. Turn out onto serving plates. Just prior to serving, preheat a broiler. Halve the figs lengthwise, drizzle each with a little of the honey, and broil for 3–4 minutes until hot and slightly browned.

Serve the panna cotta with the grilled figs and a dollop of the cream or mascarpone. Sprinkle the chopped hazelnuts on top.

Serves 6

chocolate panna cotta with
figs and hazelnuts

Light-as-air soufflés are not as difficult to make as their reputation alleges—and they more than repay the effort.

chocolate soufflé

1 1/4 cups good-quality
    dark chocolate, chopped
5 eggs, separated
1/4 cup superfine sugar, plus
    extra for dusting

2 egg whites, extra
confectioners' sugar, for dusting

Preheat the oven to 400°F. Put a cookie sheet into the oven to preheat.

Wrap a double layer of parchment paper around the outside of six 1-cup ramekins to come 1 1/2 inches above the rim and secure with string. This encourages the soufflé to rise well. Brush the insides of the ramekins with melted butter and sprinkle with superfine sugar, shaking to coat evenly and tipping out any excess. This layer of butter and sugar helps the soufflé to grip the sides and rise as it cooks.

Place the chopped chocolate in a large heatproof bowl set over a saucepan of simmering water, making sure the base of the bowl does not touch the water. Stir until the chocolate is melted and smooth, then remove the bowl from the saucepan. Stir in the egg yolks and superfine sugar.

Beat the 7 egg whites until stiff peaks form. Gently fold one-third of the egg whites into the chocolate mixture to loosen it. Then, using a metal spoon, fold in the remaining egg whites until just combined.

Spoon the mixture into the prepared ramekins and run your thumb or a blunt knife around the inside rim of the dish and the edge of the mixture. This ridge helps the soufflé to rise evenly. Place the ramekins on the preheated cookie sheet and bake for 12–15 minutes or until well risen and just set. Do not open the oven door while the soufflés are baking.

Cut the string and remove the paper collars. Lightly dust with sifted confectioners' sugar and serve immediately.

Serves 6

chocolate and almond refrigerator cake

1²/3 cups dark chocolate, chopped

1 tablespoon instant coffee granules

1 cup unsalted butter, softened

1 cup superfine sugar

1 tablespoon unsweetened cocoa powder

3 eggs, separated

1/2 cup flaked almonds, toasted

1/4 cup candied cherries, cut in half

4 cups (about 34) small almond cookies (amaretti)

2 tablespoons cognac

Line an 8¹/2-inch springform cake pan with plastic wrap.

Stirring frequently, melt the chocolate in a heatproof bowl over a saucepan of simmering water, making sure the base of the bowl does not touch the water. Stir in the coffee and leave to cool.

Beat the butter and sugar with electric beaters until light and fluffy, then sift in the cocoa powder and beat well. Add the egg yolks one at a time, beating well after each addition. Fold into the melted chocolate.

In a separate clean bowl, whisk the egg whites until stiff peaks form. Gently fold into the chocolate cream using a metal spoon. Add the almonds and cherries and fold through.

Put a tightly fitting single layer of almond cookies on the bottom of the prepared pan, flat side down. Drizzle a little cognac over them. Spread half the chocolate cream on top, then cover with another layer of cookies. Sprinkle with cognac, cover with the rest of the chocolate cream, and put a final tight layer of cookies on top, flat side down. Knock the pan on the counter a couple of times to pack the cake down. Cover the top with plastic wrap and refrigerate overnight.

Remove the cake from the pan. It will be sufficiently set to enable you to upturn it onto one hand. Peel off the plastic wrap and set it down on a serving plate, right way up. Cut into wedges to serve.

Serves 8–10

chocolate and almond
refrigerator cake

Star anise, a spice native to China, adds an exotic note that complements the other rich flavors of this dessert.

chocolate star anise cake with coffee caramel cream

1¹/3 cups good-quality dark
  chocolate, coarsely chopped
1/2 cup unsalted butter
4 eggs
2 egg yolks, extra
1/2 cup superfine sugar
1/3 cup all-purpose flour, sifted
2 teaspoons star anise, ground
1/2 cup almonds, ground

coffee caramel cream
1/2 cup heavy cream
3 tablespoons soft brown sugar
2 tablespoons brewed espresso
  coffee, cooled

Preheat the oven to 375°F. Grease a 9-inch round springform cake pan and line the bottom with parchment paper.

Put the chocolate and butter in a bowl set over a saucepan of gently simmering water, making sure the bottom of the bowl does not touch the water. Heat gently until the mixture melts.

Put the eggs, egg yolks, and sugar into a bowl and beat with electric beaters for 5 minutes until thickened. Fold in the flour, ground star anise, and ground almonds. Then fold in the melted chocolate mixture until evenly combined (the mixture should be runny at this stage).

Pour the mixture into the prepared pan and bake for 30–35 minutes or until a skewer inserted in the center comes out clean. Cool in the pan for 5 minutes, then remove and cool on a wire rack.

To make the coffee caramel cream, whip the cream, sugar, and coffee together until soft peaks form and the color is a soft caramel. Serve the cold cake cut into wedges with a spoonful of the coffee caramel cream.

Serves 8

Barbados sugar, a soft, sticky, partially refined sugar, gives a distinctive caramel taste to the topping on this torte.

chocolate and carrot torte with barbados cream

1 cup raw superfine sugar
1 cup carrot, grated (about
   2 large carrots)
1 1/2 cups self-rising flour
2 tablespoons unsweetened
   cocoa powder
2 teaspoons ground cinnamon
2 eggs, lightly beaten
3 tablespoons light olive oil
3 tablespoons whipping cream
   or buttermilk
heaping 3/4 cup dark chocolate,
   grated
3/4 cup pecans, chopped

topping
1 cup whipping cream
1 teaspoon superfine sugar
4 tablespoons thick, plain yogurt
1/4 teaspoon rum
2–3 tablespoons Barbados sugar
   or dark brown sugar

Preheat the oven to 350°F. Grease an 8-inch round springform cake pan and line the bottom with parchment paper. Put the sugar and carrot in a large bowl and mix lightly.

Sift in the flour, cocoa, and cinnamon, then add the eggs, olive oil, and cream. Stir with a wooden spoon until combined, about 30 seconds. Fold in the chocolate and pecans. Pour into the pan and bake until a skewer comes out clean when inserted in the center, 35–40 minutes. Allow to cool in the pan for 5 minutes before turning out onto a wire rack. Allow to cool completely.

Make the topping 2–3 hours before serving. Whip the cream until stiff peaks form, incorporating the superfine sugar, yogurt, and rum toward the end. Spread over the top of the cake and sprinkle the Barbados sugar over the top. Leave in a cool spot and allow the sugar to melt into a syrup. Cut into slices to serve.

Serves 8

chocolate and carrot torte with
barbados cream

chocolate ricotta layer cake

1/2 cup butter
2/3 cup superfine sugar
1 teaspoon pure vanilla extract
2 eggs, lightly beaten
1/4 cup raspberry jam
11/4 cups self-rising flour
1/2 cup unsweetened cocoa
   powder
1 teaspoon baking soda
1 cup milk

sugar syrup
2 tablespoons superfine sugar
2 tablespoons Drambuie liqueur

ricotta filling
1 cup ricotta cheese
2 tablespoons superfine sugar
2 tablespoons Drambuie liqueur

1/4 cup candied figs or apricots,
   chopped
1/4 cup candied cherries,
   chopped
2 tablespoons candied ginger
   pieces, chopped
1/3 cup dark chocolate, finely
   chopped
1/2 cup whipping cream,
   whipped to firm peaks

chocolate buttercream
heaping 3/4 cup dark chocolate,
   chopped
1/2 cup butter, chopped
2/3 cup confectioners' sugar

1/2 cup flaked almonds, toasted

Preheat the oven to 350°F. Grease an 8½-inch round cake pan and line the bottom with parchment paper. Using electric beaters, cream the butter, sugar, and vanilla in a small bowl. Add the eggs one at a time, beating well. Blend in the jam. Transfer the mixture to a larger bowl. Fold in the combined sifted flour, cocoa powder, and baking soda alternately with the milk. Pour into the pan. Bake until a skewer inserted into the center of the cake comes out clean, about 45 minutes. Leave in the pan for 15 minutes, then turn out onto a wire rack and allow to cool.

For the sugar syrup, put the sugar and 3 tablespoons water in a small saucepan. Stir to dissolve, then bring to a boil over medium heat. Boil for 1 minute, remove from the heat, and stir in the liqueur. Set aside. For the ricotta cream filling, beat together the ricotta, superfine sugar, and liqueur until smooth. Stir in the fruit and chocolate. Fold in the whipped cream. Refrigerate. For the chocolate buttercream, melt the chocolate, then set aside to cool. In a small bowl, beat the butter and confectioners' sugar with electric beaters until creamy. Beat in the cooled chocolate until thick and creamy.

To assemble, cut the cake into 3 layers. Put one layer on a serving plate. Brush with some of the sugar syrup. Spread with half the ricotta cream. Top with another cake layer, brush with syrup, and spread with the remaining ricotta cream. Brush the cut underside surface of the third layer with remaining syrup and place on top, cut side down. Spread the chocolate buttercream all over the cake. Sprinkle the top with the almonds. Refrigerate for at least 1 hour before serving.

Serves 8–10

chocolate and chestnut marquis loaf

3/4 cup dark chocolate, chopped
1/2 cup unsweetened chestnut
    purée, processed until
    smooth
1 tablespoon brandy
4 tablespoons butter
2 tablespoons unsweetened
    cocoa powder

3 tablespoons superfine sugar
2 egg yolks
1 teaspoon powdered gelatin
2/3 cup whipping cream

fresh raspberries, to serve
confectioners' sugar, to dust

Line a 2^{1}/$_{2}$ x 6^{1}/$_{2}$-inch bar pan with plastic wrap, leaving some hanging over to assist with turning out. Stirring frequently, melt the chocolate in a small heatproof bowl over a saucepan of simmering water, making sure that the bottom of the bowl does not touch the water. Remove from the heat and stir in the chestnut purée and brandy. Allow to cool.

In a medium bowl, use electric beaters to mix the butter, cocoa, and half the sugar until creamy.

In a small bowl, mix the egg yolks and remaining sugar until creamy, using electric beaters.

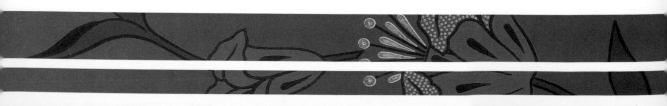

Put the gelatin in a small bowl with 2 teaspoons water. Set over a larger bowl of hot water to dissolve the gelatin.

In another bowl, beat the cream until firm, then set aside.

Using electric beaters, beat the cooled chocolate and chestnut mixture into the butter mixture until smooth. Fold in the egg mixture and gelatin, then finally fold in the beaten cream.

Pour into the prepared pan. Cover with the overlapping plastic and refrigerate for several hours or overnight.

To serve, remove the marquis from the pan with the aid of the plastic wrap. Using a hot knife, cut it into thick slices while cold and put onto serving plates. Dust the raspberries with confectioners' sugar and serve on the side.

Serves 10–12

chocolate and chestnut
marquis loaf

Try these lightly baked desserts with their molten chocolate centers for a sophisticated, adult take on comfort food.

baked chocolate desserts with rich chocolate sauce

1 1/2 tablespoons unsweetened
   cocoa powder, sifted
1 cup good-quality dark
   chocolate, chopped
1/2 cup unsalted butter, softened
3 eggs, at room temperature
2 egg yolks, extra, at room
   temperature
1/4 cup superfine sugar
3/4 cup all-purpose flour

chocolate sauce
1/2 cup good-quality dark
   chocolate, chopped
1/2 cup whipping cream

Preheat the oven to 350°F. Grease six 1/2-cup metal dariole molds and line the bottom of each with a circle of parchment paper. Dust the molds with the cocoa powder.

Put the chocolate in a small heatproof bowl over a saucepan of simmering water, making sure the bottom of the bowl doesn't touch the water.

Allow the chocolate to melt, then add the butter. When the butter has melted, stir to combine, then remove from the heat.

Beat the eggs, egg yolks, and sugar in a large bowl with electric beaters until thick, creamy, and pale. Gently fold in the chocolate mixture. Sift in the flour and gently fold through. Spoon the mixture into the molds, leaving about 1/2 inch at the top of the molds to allow the desserts to rise. Bake for 10 minutes or until the top is firm and risen.

Meanwhile, for the chocolate sauce, put the chocolate and cream in a small heatproof bowl and melt over a saucepan of simmering water, making sure the base of the bowl doesn't touch the water. Stir until melted and combined.

To serve, run a knife around the molds to loosen the desserts, then carefully turn them out onto serving plates. Drizzle with the sauce and serve immediately.

Serves 6

profiteroles with coffee mascarpone and bittersweet chocolate sauce

1 cup all-purpose flour
1/4 cup unsalted butter, cubed
1/2 teaspoon salt
4 eggs, at room temperature

filling
2 tablespoons instant coffee
  granules
2 cups mascarpone cheese
2 tablespoons confectioners'
  sugar

chocolate sauce
2/3 cup good-quality bittersweet
  chocolate, chopped
1 1/2 tablespoons unsalted butter
1/3 cup whipping cream

Preheat the oven to 400°F. Lightly grease two cookie sheets. Sift the flour onto a piece of parchment paper. Put the butter, salt, and 1 cup water into a saucepan and bring to a boil, stirring occasionally. Using the parchment paper as a funnel, pour the flour quickly into the boiling mixture. Reduce the heat to low, then beat vigorously with a wooden spoon until the mixture leaves the side of the pan and forms a smooth ball. Transfer the mixture to a bowl and set aside to cool until lukewarm. Using electric beaters, beat in the eggs, one at a time, until the mixture is thick and glossy.

Using two spoons, gently drop 16 rounded balls of the mixture about 1¼ inches in diameter and 1¼ inches apart onto the prepared cookie sheets. Bake for 20 minutes or until the balls are puffed. Reduce the heat to 350°F and bake for 10 minutes more or until the puffs are golden brown and crisp.

Using a small sharp knife, gently slit the puffs to allow the steam to escape, then return them to the oven for 10 minutes or until the insides are dry. Allow to cool to room temperature.

Meanwhile, to make the filling, dissolve the instant coffee in 1 tablespoon boiling water. Set aside to cool. Beat the coffee, mascarpone, and confectioners' sugar until just combined. Be careful not to overmix or the mascarpone mixture will separate.

To make the bittersweet chocolate sauce, put the chocolate, butter, and cream in a small heatproof bowl over a saucepan of simmering water, making sure the bottom of the bowl doesn't touch the water. Stir until combined. Set aside to cool slightly.

Just before serving, slit the profiteroles in half and sandwich together with the filling. Drizzle with the chocolate sauce or serve the sauce separately.

Makes 16

profiteroles with coffee mascarpone
and dark chocolate sauce

chocolate, hazelnut, and orange dessert cake with blood orange sauce

1¹/₃ cups good-quality
   bittersweet chocolate,
   chopped
1¹/₂ cups blanched hazelnuts
heaping ³/₄ cup unsalted butter,
   softened
³/₄ cup superfine sugar
4 eggs, at room temperature,
   separated
3 teaspoons espresso instant
   coffee granules
zest of 1 orange, finely grated

heaping ³/₄ cup cornstarch
confectioners' sugar,
   to dust
heavy cream, to serve

blood orange syrup
1 cup strained blood orange
   juice (from 4–5 oranges)
¹/₄ cup superfine sugar
1 teaspoon orange liqueur, such
   as Cointreau (optional)

Preheat the oven to 325°F. Grease an 8-inch round springform cake pan.

Put the chocolate in a heatproof bowl and place the bowl over a saucepan of simmering water, making sure the bottom of the bowl doesn't touch the water. Stirring occasionally, heat until melted.

Put the hazelnuts in a food processor and process until finely chopped. Cream the butter and superfine sugar in a large bowl with electric beaters until pale and fluffy. Add the egg yolks, one at a time, beating well after each addition. Gently stir in the melted chocolate, coffee granules, and orange zest. Mix in the cornstarch and chopped hazelnuts.

Whisk the egg whites until soft peaks form. Using a large metal spoon, fold a scoop of egg white into the chocolate mixture. Gently fold in the remaining egg white. Spoon the mixture into the prepared pan and level the surface. Bake for 30 minutes, then cover loosely with foil and bake for another 40–45 minutes or until a skewer inserted into the center of the cake comes out clean. Don't be too concerned if the surface cracks.

Meanwhile, for the blood orange syrup, put the strained orange juice and sugar in a small saucepan and stir over low heat until the sugar dissolves. Bring to a boil, then reduce the heat and simmer for 10–12 minutes or until reduced by half. Stir in the liqueur, if using, and set aside to cool slightly.

To serve, cut the warm cake into slices. Lightly dust with confectioners' sugar, spoon over a little of the warm orange syrup, and serve with cream.

Serves 6–8

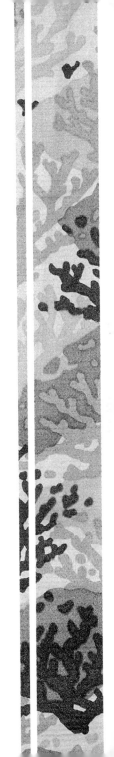

black and white chocolate pie

pastry
6 1/2 tablespoons unsalted
    butter, at room temperature
1/4 cup superfine sugar
1 egg, at room temperature,
    lightly beaten
1 1/2 cups all-purpose flour
1/4 cup self-rising flour
1 tablespoon unsweetened
    cocoa powder

filling
2 teaspoons powdered gelatin
3/4 cup milk
1/2 cup superfine sugar

1/2 cup good-quality white
    chocolate, chopped
4 egg yolks, at room
    temperature, lightly beaten
1 cup whipping cream, whipped
    to soft peaks

chocolate glaze
1/4 cup whipping cream
1/2 cup good-quality dark
    chocolate, chopped
2 teaspoons unsalted butter,
    cubed
2 teaspoons light corn syrup

Preheat the oven to 375°F. Lightly grease the sides of an 8-inch springform cake pan and line the bottom with parchment paper.

For the pastry, beat the butter with an electric beater until smooth and fluffy. Beat in the sugar and egg until combined. Sift in the combined flours and cocoa and stir until the dough comes together. Knead briefly on a lightly floured surface until smooth. Flatten into a disk, wrap in plastic wrap, and refrigerate for 30 minutes. Roll the pastry between two sheets of parchment paper until about $1/2$ inch thick, and trim to fit the base of the pan. Ease the pastry into the pan, removing the paper, and lightly prick with a fork. Bake for 15 minutes or until slightly firm to the touch. Set aside to cool.

For the filling, combine the gelatin and 2 tablespoons water in a small bowl and set aside for 2 minutes to absorb and swell. Heat the milk, sugar, and chocolate in a saucepan until simmering. Stir until the sugar dissolves and the chocolate melts. Put the egg yolks in a bowl and whisk in the warm chocolate mixture. Return the mixture to a clean saucepan and stir over medium heat until it lightly coats the back of a spoon. Add the gelatin mixture and stir until dissolved. Transfer to a bowl, place over a bowl of ice, and beat until cold. Fold in the cream. Pour the mixture over the pastry and refrigerate overnight or until set.

For the glaze, put the cream, chocolate, butter, and corn syrup in a saucepan and stir over low–medium heat until smooth. Cool until thickened. Remove the pie from the pan and spoon the glaze over the top, allowing it to drip down the sides. Use a metal spatula to smooth the glaze over the top of the pie. Set aside at room temperature for 1 hour or until the glaze sets.

Serves 12

black and white chocolate pie

Self-saucing pudding cakes are a bit of kitchen magic: the sauce goes in on the top but—presto!—ends up on the bottom.

chocolate and cinnamon pudding cakes

$1/3$ cup good-quality dark
   chocolate, chopped
$1/4$ cup unsalted butter, cubed
2 tablespoons unsweetened
   cocoa powder, sifted
$2/3$ cup milk
1 cup self-rising flour
$1/2$ cup superfine sugar
$1/3$ cup soft brown sugar, firmly
   packed
1 egg, at room temperature,
   lightly beaten
heavy cream, to serve

cinnamon sauce
$1 1/2$ teaspoons ground
   cinnamon
$1/4$ cup unsalted butter, cubed
$1/3$ cup soft brown sugar, firmly
   packed
$1/4$ cup unsweetened cocoa
   powder, sifted

Preheat the oven to 350°F. Grease four 1-cup ovenproof ramekins.

Combine the chocolate, butter, cocoa, and milk in a saucepan. Stir over low heat until the chocolate melts. Remove from the heat.

Sift the flour into a large bowl and stir in the sugars. Add to the chocolate mixture with the egg and mix well. Spoon the mixture into the prepared dishes, put on a cookie sheet, and set aside while you make the sauce.

For the cinnamon sauce, combine the cinnamon, butter, brown sugar, cocoa, and 1$1/2$ cups water in a small saucepan. Stir over low heat until combined. Carefully pour the sauce onto the puddings over the back of a spoon. Bake for 40 minutes or until firm. Turn out the puddings and serve with heavy cream.

Serves 4

chocolate ravioli

filling
scant 1/2 cup good-quality dark
    chocolate, chopped
2 tablespoons unsalted butter,
    cubed
3 tablespoons whipping cream

dough
2 cups all-purpose flour
1/2 teaspoon baking powder
2 teaspoons superfine sugar

1/4 teaspoon salt
1 egg
1/3 cup light olive oil
2 1/2 tablespoons dry white wine

1 egg, lightly beaten
vegetable oil, for deep-frying
confectioners' sugar, to dust
1/2 cup maple syrup, to serve
    (optional)

For the filling, melt the chocolate, butter, and cream in a small bowl over a saucepan of simmering water, making sure the bottom of the bowl does not touch the water. Stir until smooth and glossy. Remove the bowl from the heat, cool, and refrigerate until solid.

For the dough, put the flour, baking powder, sugar, and salt in a food processor. Process in short bursts until just combined. Combine the egg, oil, and wine in a pitcher. Gradually pour into the processor while the motor is running, then stop processing when the mixture starts to clump together. Transfer to a lightly floured surface and knead until smooth, 3–4 minutes. Cover with plastic wrap and refrigerate for 30 minutes.

Roll the dough out to $1/10$-inch thickness. Cover with a dish towel and allow to rest while you shape the filling.

Using a teaspoon or a small melon baller, scoop out rounded teaspoonfuls of the chocolate filling. They don't need to be perfectly round, but in a solid lump. If the kitchen is hot, keep the balls in the refrigerator and take out a few at a time as needed. You will need 18 balls.

With a cookie cutter or a glass, cut $3^1/4$-inch circles from the dough. Brush around the rims of a few circles with a little beaten egg. Place a chocolate ball in the center of each. Fold the dough over to encase it, forming a half-moon shape. Press the edges together firmly to seal. Put on a tray and refrigerate while you make the rest of the ravioli.

Half-fill a deep saucepan with oil and heat until hot but not smoking, 350°F. Fry the ravioli, a few at a time, until puffed and golden brown, about $1^1/2$ minutes. Drain on crumpled paper towels, then dust liberally with confectioners' sugar. Serve warm while the chocolate center is still melted, accompanied by a small bowl of maple syrup for dipping.

Makes 18

chocolate ravioli

This dark, dense, delectable cake is proof that the most delicious recipes need not be complicated.

dark chocolate pecan torte

3 cups pecans
1²/₃ cups dark chocolate, chopped
scant 1¹/₄ cup butter, cubed

4 eggs, separated
1 cup superfine sugar
2 tablespoons brandy
whipped cream, to serve

Preheat the oven to 315°F. Grease a 10-inch springform cake pan and line the bottom with parchment paper.

In a food processor, process the pecans until finely chopped. Stirring, heat the chocolate and butter in a bowl over a saucepan of simmering water until just melted. Set aside.

Using electric beaters, beat the egg yolks and sugar in a large bowl until thick and pale, about 2 minutes. Slowly beat in the melted chocolate mixture, then use a metal spoon to fold in the pecans.

In a separate clean bowl, beat the egg whites to firm peaks. Fold in one-third of the egg whites into the chocolate to loosen the mixture, then lightly fold in the remainder. Spoon into the prepared pan and smooth the surface.

Bake for 10 minutes. Reduce the temperature to 300°F and bake until set and firm to the touch, another 45 minutes. Sprinkle the brandy over the cake while it is still warm. Allow the cake to cool completely in the pan before removing.

Cut into wedges and serve warm, cold, or chilled with whipped cream.

Serves 10–12

mocha coconut cakes

1/2 cup unsalted butter,
    chopped and softened
1 cup superfine sugar
1/2 teaspoon pure vanilla extract
2 eggs
2 cups self-rising flour
1 cup milk
2 teaspoons instant coffee,
    dissolved in 2 teaspoons
    boiling water

frosting
3 cups confectioners' sugar
1/2 cup unsweetened cocoa
    powder
1 1/2 tablespoons unsalted butter
2 teaspoons instant coffee
    powder
1 1/4 cups shredded sweetened
    coconut
1 cup dried grated sweetened
    coconut

Preheat the oven to 350°F. Lightly grease the base of a 9-inch square shallow pan and line the bottom with parchment paper.

Using electric beaters, cream the butter, sugar, and vanilla in a bowl until pale and fluffy. Add the eggs one at a time, beating well after each addition. Sift the flour into the butter mixture alternately with the milk until combined and smooth. Spoon half the mixture into the prepared pan and spread evenly over the bottom. Add the dissolved coffee to the remaining mixture and stir until well combined. Carefully spread the coffee mixture over the mixture in the pan.

Bake for 30–35 minutes or until a skewer inserted into the center of the cake comes out clean. Cool in the pan for 5 minutes before turning out onto a wire rack to cool completely.

Cut the cake into 25 squares.

For the frosting, sift the confectioners' sugar and cocoa powder into a large shallow bowl. Add the butter and coffee and gradually whisk in $2/3$ cup boiling water until smooth. Put the shredded and grated coconuts in a large shallow bowl and toss to combine.

Using two spoons to hold the cake, dip the cake squares into the frosting to cover, allowing the excess to drip off. (Add a little boiling water to the frosting if it starts to thicken). Roll the cake in the coconut to cover and place on a wire rack. Repeat with the remaining cakes.

Makes 25

dreamy and creamy Smooth, silky, and delicately pretty, these desserts hark back to a time when life was a little less rushed and meals were a little less expedient, when eating wasn't a matter of

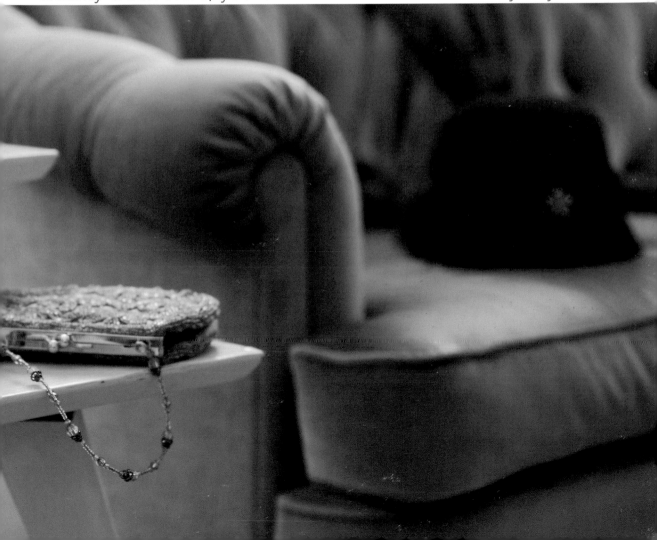

wolfing down a meal, then rushing off, but lingering over good conversation and a last, indulgent spoonful of a homemade creamy treat. Here, you can rediscover those dreamy days indeed.

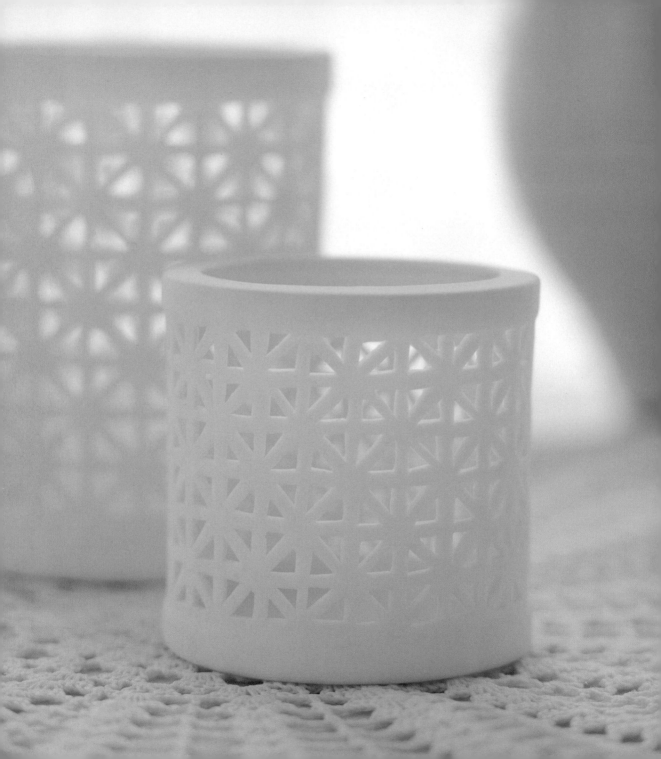

Heavy cream, whipping cream, custard, cream cheese, panna cotta, mascarpone, crème fraîche, crème anglaise—the list could go on! Cream in all its glorious forms and creations is the star of this chapter. From the classic heart-shaped dessert *coeur à la crème* to rich mocha coffee cream pots and fragrant panna cotta phyllo with rose-water syrup and pistachios, cream has been adding a touch of luxury to desserts and cakes for a very long, happy time. Unlike the boldness of chocolate desserts or the fresh vitality of fruit-based sweets, creamy concoctions invite a more gentle, unhurried approach to cooking and sharing food. For the cook, pleasure can be found in the presentation of such pretty desserts—lace and filigree, the good glassware, and pressed linen napkins all seem to be required. And for the lucky diner, certainly, it's hard to rush off when faced with the silky seductiveness of a crème caramel or a cardamom kulfi. Appropriately for such a well-loved ingredient, this chapter contains many familiar recipes such as lemon pie and tiramisu, as well as many contemporary recipes, such as honeycomb and mascarpone cheesecake. Creamy desserts are defined by their all-together too-smooth texture. Yet if textures are wonderfully uniform, flavors are surprisingly varied. Honey, coffee, alcohol, fruit, and nuts, as well as spices and perfumes such as vanilla, cinnamon, ginger, and flower waters, all add depth and flavor to these desserts. Sophisticated, subtle, festive—cream truly deserves its place at the heart of many classic recipes. Who wouldn't linger over such desserts?

coeur à la crème with blueberry coulis

1 cup farmer cheese or
　　Neufchâtel
1/2 cup confectioners' sugar
1/4 teaspoon pure vanilla extract
1 cup whipping cream

blueberry coulis
1 cup fresh blueberries
1 tablespoon superfine sugar
1 teaspoon lemon juice
1 teaspoon crème de cassis
　　(black currant liqueur),
　　optional

crystallized fruits
1 small bunch each green and
　　purple seedless grapes
　　(about 25 grapes) (see note)
2 egg whites, lightly whisked
1/4 cup superfine sugar

Line one large or four individual coeur à la crème molds (see note) with cheesecloth. Put the cheese, confectioners' sugar, and vanilla in a food processor and process until smooth. In a large bowl, whip the cream until firm peaks form. Fold the cheese mixture through the cream.

Spoon the mixture into the prepared mold and pack down tightly. Cover the mold and set it on a deep plate. Put in the refrigerator and leave for 12 hours or overnight to drain.

For the blueberry coulis, process the blueberries and sugar in a food processor until smooth and glossy. Strain through a fine sieve into a small bowl, pressing the pulp through. Stir in the lemon juice and liqueur.

For the crystallized fruits, brush each piece with egg white. While still wet, dip into the sugar and put on a tray lined with parchment paper to dry.

To serve, remove the coeurs from their molds and place onto a serving plate. Gently peel off the cheesecloth. Spoon a little coulis over and around each and pile the crystallized fruits on top.

Notes: Coeur à la crème molds are heart-shaped, with holes in the bottom to allow for drainage of the liquid (whey) from the cheese mixture with which they are filled. If you can't obtain a large mold, use 4 individual ones. Choose small grapes for decoration so that they don't dwarf the coeur. When available, fresh black or white currants in little bunches also work well.

Serves 4

meringue sandwiches with passion fruit cream and raspberries

2 egg whites
heaping 1 cup superfine sugar
1/2 teaspoon pure vanilla extract
1/2 teaspoon cornstarch

passion fruit cream
1/2 cup whipping cream
4 tablespoons passion fruit pulp
   (from 2 large passion fruit)

macadamia toffee shards
1/3 cup roasted, unsalted
   macadamia nuts
scant 1/2 cup superfine sugar

passion fruit liqueur sauce
3 tablespoons strained passion
   fruit juice (from 6 large
   passion fruit)
1 tablespoon superfine sugar
2 teaspoons cornstarch
1 tablespoon Grand Marnier
   or other orange liqueur

1/2 cup whipping cream, extra
1 tablespoon confectioners'
   sugar
1/2 cup fresh raspberries

Preheat the oven to 260°F. Line a large cookie sheet with parchment paper. In a large bowl, beat the egg whites with electric beaters until firm peaks form. Gradually add the sugar. Beat for 3 minutes until the sugar dissolves and the meringue is glossy and thick. Beat in the vanilla and cornstarch. Put eight spoonfuls of the mixture evenly spaced onto the tray and flatten each slightly to a 3$1/4$-inch freeform circle. Bake until crisp on the outside, about 40 minutes. Turn off the oven and leave the meringues to cool in the oven with the door ajar.

For the passion fruit cream, whip the cream in a small bowl until firm peaks form. Fold in the passion fruit pulp until smooth. Chill. For the toffee, roughly chop the macadamias and put on a lightly greased sheet. Put the sugar and 3 tablespoons water in a small saucepan. Stir until the sugar dissolves, then increase the heat. Boil without stirring until the mixture caramelizes, 4–5 minutes. Pour over the nuts and leave to harden. Break into pieces. Store in an airtight container until needed.

For the sauce, combine the passion fruit juice, sugar, and cornstarch in a small saucepan. Stir over low heat until thickened. Remove from the heat and stir in the liqueur. Set aside but do not refrigerate. Whip the extra cream with 1 tablespoon confectioners' sugar until thick.

To assemble, put four meringues onto large serving plates. Spread the passion fruit cream over each. Top with the remaining meringues, then the whipped cream, passion fruit liqueur sauce, and a few raspberries. Decorate each sandwich with a shard of toffee and serve immediately.

Serves 4

meringue sandwiches with passion
fruit cream and raspberries

crème caramel

1/2 cup superfine sugar
2 2/3 cups milk
1 vanilla bean

scant 2/3 cup superfine sugar
3 eggs, beaten
3 egg yolks, extra

Preheat the oven to 350°F.

Heat the sugar in a heavy-bottom saucepan until it dissolves and starts to caramelize—tip the pan from side to side as the sugar cooks to keep the coloring even. Remove from the heat and carefully add 2 tablespoons water to stop the cooking process (be aware that the toffee will splatter). Pour into six 1/2-cup ramekins and leave to cool.

Put the milk and vanilla bean in a saucepan and bring just to a boil. Mix together the sugar, egg, and egg yolks. Strain the boiling milk over the egg mixture and stir well. Ladle into the ramekins and place in a baking pan. Pour enough hot water into the pan to come halfway up the sides of the ramekins. Cook for 35–40 minutes or until firm to the touch. Remove from the pan and leave for 15 minutes. Remove from the molds and place onto plates. Pour on any leftover caramel.

Serves 6

tiramisu

3 cups strong black coffee, cooled
3 tablespoons brandy or Kahlùa
2 eggs, separated
3 tablespoons superfine sugar
1 cup mascarpone cheese

1 cup whipping cream, whipped
16 large Italian ladyfingers (savoiardi)
2 teaspoons dark unsweetened cocoa powder

Combine the coffee and brandy or Kahlùa in a bowl. Using electric beaters, beat the egg yolks and sugar in a medium bowl for 3 minutes or until thick and pale. Add the mascarpone and beat until just combined. Fold in the whipped cream with a metal spoon. Beat the egg whites until soft peaks form. Fold quickly and lightly into the cream mixture with a metal spoon, trying not to lose the volume.

Dip half the ladyfingers, one at a time, into the coffee mixture, each for about 2 seconds. Drain off any excess and arrange the ladyfingers in the base of a deep 5-cup serving dish. Spread half the cream mixture over the ladyfingers. Dip the remaining ladyfingers and repeat the layers. Discard the leftover coffee mixture. Smooth the surface and dust liberally with cocoa powder. Refrigerate for at least 2 hours or until firm.

Serves 6–8

individual panettone puddings

3/4 cup milk
3/4 cup whipping cream
1 teaspoon pure vanilla extract
3 eggs

1/2 cup superfine sugar
about 7 ounces panettone
1/2 cup golden raisins
custard or crème anglaise,
    to serve

Preheat the oven to 300°F. Grease eight 1/2-cup timbale molds with butter. Combine the milk, cream, and vanilla in a saucepan, heat until almost boiling, then remove from the heat. Whisk the eggs and sugar in a bowl until pale and thick, then gradually add the cream mixture, whisking to combine well. Cut the panettone into 1/2-inch-thick slices, and then cut out 16 rounds using a 2-inch cutter. Place a round in the bottom of each mold, sprinkle over the raisins, then pour 1/4 cup of the custard mixture over each. Top with another round and enough custard mixture to cover the panettone and fill the mold. Put the puddings in a large baking dish and pour in hot water to come halfway up the sides of the molds. Bake for 25–30 minutes or until golden and firm. Remove the molds from the hot water, allow to cool for 5 minutes, then invert onto serving plates. Serve with the custard or crème anglaise.

Makes 8

mocha coffee cream pots

2 cups whipping cream
$2/3$ cup roasted coffee beans
$2/3$ cup dark chocolate, chopped
6 egg yolks
$1/4$ cup superfine sugar
3 teaspoons Tia Maria or other
    coffee liqueur

whipped cream, to serve
chocolate-covered coffee beans,
    to serve

Preheat the oven to 300°F. Put the cream, coffee beans, and chocolate into a medium saucepan. Stir over low heat until the chocolate melts, then bring to a simmer and cook for 2–3 minutes. Remove from the heat. Allow to stand for 30 minutes to allow the coffee to infuse.

Whisk the egg yolks, sugar, and liqueur together in a bowl, then strain in the coffee-infused milk, discarding the coffee beans. Stir to combine, then divide the mixture among six $1/2$-cup ramekins or ovenproof teacups. Put in a baking dish with high sides and add enough hot water to come halfway up the sides of the ramekins. Bake for 25–30 minutes. Remove from the oven and cool. Refrigerate overnight until set.

Serve in the pots with whipped cream and chocolate-covered coffee beans.

Serves 6

mocha coffee cream pots

panna cotta phyllo with rose-water syrup and pistachios

1 1/2 teaspoons powdered
    gelatin
2 cups whipping cream
1 cup unsweetened yogurt
2/3 cup superfine sugar
1 vanilla bean

phyllo shells
4 sheets phyllo pastry
unsalted butter, for brushing
2 tablespoons superfine sugar

rose-water syrup
1/2 cup superfine sugar
1 cinnamon stick
1/2 teaspoon rose water
1 drop rose-pink food coloring
    (optional)

2 tablespoons pistachio nuts,
    chopped and roasted

For the panna cotta, put 2 tablespoons water in a small bowl, sprinkle with the powdered gelatin, and set aside for 2 minutes to absorb and swell. Put the cream, yogurt, and sugar in a saucepan. Split the vanilla bean lengthwise and scrape the seeds into the saucepan, discarding the pod. Stir the mixture over low heat until the sugar dissolves. Add the gelatin to the saucepan and stir until the gelatin dissolves. Pour the mixture into six 1/2-cup moulds. Refrigerate for 5 hours or until set.

Meanwhile, preheat the oven to 375°F. Lightly brush a sheet of phyllo pastry with the melted butter. Sprinkle one-third of the sugar over the pastry, top with another sheet of pastry, and press down gently to stick the pastry together. Repeat this process for four layers of pastry. Using a sharp knife, cut six 4^1/$_2$-inch square pieces from the pastry. Line a 6-cup giant muffin pan with the pastry squares. Line each pastry shell with a square of parchment paper and weigh it down with pastry weights or uncooked rice. Bake for 2 minutes, then remove the paper and weights and bake for an additional 2–3 minutes or until lightly golden. Cool the pastry shells on a wire rack.

For the rose-water syrup, put ^{3}/$_4$ cup water, the sugar, and cinnamon stick in a small saucepan. Stir over low heat until the sugar dissolves. Increase the heat to high and simmer for 3–4 minutes or until slightly syrupy. Add the rose water and food coloring, if using. Remove from the heat and set aside to cool. When cool, remove the cinnamon stick.

Run a spatula or blunt knife around the panna cotta, then carefully invert them into the pastry shells. Drizzle the panna cotta with the rose-water syrup and sprinkle with the pistachios.

Serves 6

festive cannoli

cannoli
1¼ cups all-purpose flour
1 tablespoon superfine sugar
1½ tablespoons cold butter,
    cubed
3 tablespoons white wine
1 teaspoon white wine vinegar

1 egg white, lightly beaten
vegetable oil, for deep-frying

ricotta filling
3 cups ricotta cheese
2 tablespoons superfine sugar

3 teaspoons rose water or
    orange flower water
scant ¼ cup mixed candied
    fruits, chopped
scant ¼ cup candied citrus peel,
    finely chopped
1½ tablespoons dark chocolate,
    chopped

confectioners' sugar, to dust

For the cannoli, put the flour and sugar in a bowl and add the butter. Use your fingertips to rub in the butter until the mixture resembles fine bread crumbs. Add the wine and vinegar and mix to a rough dough.

Turn out onto a floured surface and knead for 5 minutes until smooth and elastic. Wrap in plastic wrap and refrigerate for 2 hours. Divide the dough into 16 even-sized pieces. Roll each piece into a 4-inch round. Wrap each piece around a cannoli cylinder (see note) and seal closed with egg white. Press to ensure it adheres firmly.

Put enough oil in a medium saucepan to come halfway up the sides. Heat over medium heat to 350°F on a candy thermometer. Deep-fry 2 to 3 tubes at a time until evenly golden brown, 1–1½ minutes. Drain on paper towels; remove the cylinders while still warm. Set aside to cool and crisp.

For the ricotta filling, beat the ricotta and sugar with a fork in a medium bowl until smooth and creamy. Stir in the rose water, candied fruits, peel, and chocolate.

Use a teaspoon to fill the pastries from both ends. Stack the cannoli high on a large serving platter and dust liberally with confectioners' sugar. Serve at once.

Notes: Cannoli cylinders are special metal cylinders that can be found in kitchenware stores. Buy fresh ricotta sold in bulk at delicatessens and specialty cheese stores. It has a much better texture and flavor than the type sold in tubs.

Makes 16

festive cannoli

For a really good chocolate sauce, use fine-quality bittersweet chocolate with 50–70 percent cocoa solids.

coffee crémets with chocolate sauce

1 cup cream cheese
1 cup heavy cream
4 tablespoons very strong coffee
$1/3$ cup superfine sugar

chocolate sauce
$2/3$ cup dark chocolate
$3^1/2$ tablespoons unsalted butter

Line four $1/2$-cup ramekins with plastic wrap, leaving enough hanging over the side to wrap over the crémet. Beat the cream cheese a little until smooth, then whisk in the cream. Mix in the coffee and sugar. Spoon into the ramekins and fold the plastic wrap over the top. Refrigerate for at least $1^1/2$ hours, then unwrap, turn the crémets out onto serving plates, and carefully peel off the plastic wrap.

For the sauce, gently melt the chocolate, butter, and 4 tablespoons water in a saucepan. Stir well until shiny, then let the sauce cool a little. Pour a little chocolate sauce over each crémet.

Serves 4

cardamom and yogurt bavarian cream

4 egg yolks
1/2 cup superfine sugar
3/4 cup vanilla yogurt
3/4 cup milk
1 teaspoon ground cardamom

1/2 teaspoon pure vanilla extract
1 tablespoon powdered gelatin
1 cup whipping cream

Beat the egg yolks and sugar until thick and pale. Combine the yogurt, milk, cardamom, and vanilla in a saucepan and stir over low heat until just coming to a simmer. Pour the warm milk mixture over the yolks and whisk to combine. Return to a clean saucepan and stir over medium heat for 7–8 minutes or until the custard thickens enough to coat the back of a wooden spoon. Remove from the heat.

Dissolve the gelatin in 3 tablespoons hot water and stir it through the custard. Set the custard aside to cool completely. Whip the cream until soft peaks form, then gently fold the cream through the cooled custard.

Divide the mixture among eight 1/2-cup molds and refrigerate for 2–3 hours to set. To remove from the mold, dip a blunt knife into warm water and run the tip around the edge of the mold. Dip the mold into a bowl of warm water for a few seconds, shaking slightly to loosen. Place the serving plate over the mold, invert, and remove the mold.

Makes 8

passion fruit swirl layer cake

sponge cake
2 eggs
1/3 cup superfine sugar
1/2 cup all-purpose flour
2 tablespoons cornstarch
1/2 teaspoon baking powder

passion fruit filling
1 tablespoon powdered gelatin
1 1/2 cups cream cheese,
   softened
1/2 cup superfine sugar
1 teaspoon pure vanilla extract

1/2 pint whipping cream,
   whipped
6 tablespoons strained passion
   fruit juice (from 9–10 fresh
   passion fruit)
few drops egg-yellow food
   coloring

1/2 pint whipping cream, extra,
   whipped
1 cup sweetened shredded
   coconut, toasted
pulp of 1 passion fruit, to serve

Preheat the oven to 350°F. Grease an 8 1/2-inch round springform cake pan and line the bottom with parchment paper.

For the cake, beat the eggs in a medium bowl with electric beaters on high speed until pale and thick, about 3 minutes. Add the sugar and beat for 1 minute. Sift in the flour, cornstarch, and baking powder, then gently fold into the egg mixture with a metal spoon. Pour into the prepared pan and bake in the center of the oven until a skewer inserted into the center comes out clean, 15–20 minutes. Cool in the pan for 5 minutes, then turn out onto a wire rack to cool completely. Clean the cake pan.

For the filling, mix the gelatin with 2 tablespoons cold water in a small bowl. Put over a bowl of hot water and stir until dissolved. Set aside. In a large bowl, beat the cream cheese, sugar, and vanilla until light and creamy. Stir in the gelatin mixture, then fold in the whipped cream. Spoon half the filling into another bowl. Mix in the passion fruit juice and enough drops of food coloring to give a good passion fruit color.

To assemble, slice the sponge cake in half. In the cleaned cake pan, lay two long strips of parchment paper across each other to use as handles to remove the cake later. Put a layer of sponge cake in the bottom and dollop in both the passion fruit and plain cheesecake mixtures. Use a teaspoon to gently swirl the mixtures together. Put the second layer of sponge cake on top, pressing down gently. Chill for 2–3 hours or until firm.

Transfer to a serving plate, using the parchment paper strips for leverage. Spread the whipped cream over the top and sides of the cake, making deep swirls on top. Press the coconut into the sides, and top with the passion fruit pulp.

Serves 10–12

passion fruit swirl layer cake

lemon pie

pastry
1 1/2 cups all-purpose flour
1/2 cup confectioners' sugar
1/3 cup almonds, ground
9 tablespoons unsalted butter,
    chilled and cubed
1 egg yolk, at room
    temperature

filling
1 1/2 tablespoons lemon zest,
    finely grated
1/3 cup lemon juice, strained
5 eggs, at room temperature
3/4 cup superfine sugar
1/2 pint whipping cream

confectioners' sugar, for dusting
heavy cream, to serve

For the pastry, put the flour, confectioners' sugar, ground almonds, and butter in a food processor and process until the mixture resembles fine crumbs. Add the egg yolk and process until the dough just comes together. Knead gently and briefly on a lightly floured surface until the dough is smooth. Form into a ball, flatten into a disk, cover with plastic wrap, and refrigerate for 30 minutes.

Preheat the oven to 350°F. Grease an 8 1/2-inch loose-bottom pie pan. Roll out the pastry between two sheets of parchment paper to a thickness of 1/8 inch to cover the base and sides of the pan. Peel off the top sheet of parchment paper, carefully invert the pastry into the pan, and peel off the second sheet of paper. Press the pastry gently into the base and sides, ensuring the pastry is level with the top of the pan. Trim off any excess pastry. Refrigerate for 10 minutes.

Line the pastry with a sheet of parchment paper and pour in some pastry weights or uncooked rice or beans. Place the pan on a cookie sheet and bake for 10 minutes. Remove the paper and weights and return to the oven for another 10–15 minutes or until light golden. Set aside to cool. Reduce the heat to 275°F.

To make the filling, put the lemon zest, lemon juice, eggs, sugar, and cream in a bowl and whisk until combined. Set aside for 10 minutes to allow the lemon zest to infuse the mixture, then strain the mixture. Carefully pour the filling into the pastry shell and bake for 45–50 minutes or until just set. Set aside to cool for 10 minutes, then refrigerate until cold. Dust the pie with confectioners' sugar and serve with heavy cream.

Serves 6–8

These delicate little towers of pecan-flavored creamy custard will please both the palate and the eye.

pecan bavarian with baileys cream

1 2/3 cups pecans
1 1/2 tablespoons gelatin
3/4 cup milk
2/3 cup superfine sugar
6 egg yolks
1 1/2 teaspoons pure vanilla
   extract
1 1/2 cups whipping cream
sweetened instant cocoa,
   to serve

Baileys cream
1/2 cup whipping cream
2 teaspoons Baileys Original
   Irish Cream liqueur

Preheat the broiler to medium-high. Spread the pecans on a cookie sheet and put under the broiler until lightly toasted. Cool, then grind in a food processor until fine. Put the gelatin in a small glass bowl and stir in 1 1/2 tablespoons cold water. Support the bowl in a larger bowl of boiling water and stir until dissolved.

Put the milk in a small saucepan and bring to just below boiling point. Remove from the heat. In the top of a double saucepan over boiling water, whisk the sugar and egg yolks until pale, then gradually add the milk, whisking continuously. Stirring, continue cooking until the mixture thickens. Remove from the heat and stir in the gelatin, ground pecans, and vanilla. Cool for 10 minutes, then chill until just starting to set.

Lightly oil six tall 2/3-cup dariole molds. Whip the cream until soft peaks form and fold into the pecan mixture. Spoon into the prepared molds and return to the refrigerator to set overnight.

For the Baileys cream, whip the cream until soft peaks form, then stir in the Baileys.

To serve, remove the Bavarians from the molds and place onto serving plates. Sift some instant cocoa over the tops and spoon some Baileys cream around the Bavarians. Serve at once.

Serves 6

pecan bavarian with baileys cream

honeycomb and mascarpone cheesecake

1 cup graham cracker crumbs
5 tablespoons unsalted butter,
    melted
1¹/2 teaspoons powdered
    gelatin
¹/2 pint whipping cream
2 eggs, separated, at room
    temperature
1 cup mascarpone cheese
¹/3 cup superfine sugar

1 teaspoon pure vanilla extract
1 chocolate-coated honeycomb
    candy bar, crushed (to yield
    about ¹/2 cup)

white chocolate sauce
heaping ³/4 cup good-quality
    white chocolate, chopped
¹/3 cup whipping cream

Lightly grease the base of an 8-inch round springform cake pan.

Put the melted butter in a small bowl, add the cracker crumbs, and stir to combine. Press the mixture into the base of the cake pan. Refrigerate for 15 minutes.

Put 2 tablespoons water in a small bowl, sprinkle with the powdered gelatin, and set aside for 2 minutes to absorb and swell.

Meanwhile, heat the cream in a small saucepan until it reaches simmering point. Remove the saucepan from the heat. Add the gelatin mixture to the saucepan and stir until the gelatin dissolves. Set aside to cool.

Beat the egg yolks, mascarpone, 1/4 cup of the sugar, and the vanilla in a small bowl with electric beaters until smooth. Fold in the crushed honeycomb. Add the cream mixture and mix well.

Beat the egg whites and remaining sugar until stiff peaks form. Fold into the mascarpone mixture with a metal spoon, then pour into the pan over the base and refrigerate overnight.

To make the white chocolate sauce, put the white chocolate and cream in a small heatproof bowl and place over a small saucepan of simmering water, making sure the base of the bowl doesn't touch the water. Stir until melted and smooth, then set aside to cool slightly. To serve, cut the cheesecake into slices and drizzle with the white chocolate sauce.

Serves 8

This variation on the classic French custard gains a tropical zing with the addition of coconut and fresh ginger.

coconut and ginger crème brûlée

2 cups whipping cream
1/3 cup sweetened shredded
   coconut
1 tablespoon fresh ginger, finely
   grated

4 egg yolks, at room
   temperature
1/4 cup superfine sugar
2 tablespoons turbinado sugar

Preheat the oven to 315°F.

Put the cream, shredded coconut, and ginger in a saucepan. Stirring, slowly heat the mixture until it is just below boiling point. Strain into a bowl, pressing on the solids to extract all the liquid. Discard the solids.

Using electric beaters, whisk the egg yolks and superfine sugar in a heatproof bowl until thick and pale, about 5 minutes. Gradually whisk in the hot cream. Place the bowl over a saucepan of barely simmering water, making sure that the bottom of the bowl does not touch the water.

Stir the mixture over the simmering water for about 10 minutes or until it thickens slightly and coats the back of a spoon.

Put four ½-cup ovenproof dishes in a baking pan and divide the cream mixture among the dishes. Add enough boiling water to the baking pan to come three-quarters of the way up the sides of the dishes. Bake for 20–25 minutes or until the custards are just set. Carefully remove the dishes from the water and set aside to cool to room temperature, then cover and refrigerate for 3 hours.

Preheat the broiler to high. Put the custards in a shallow baking pan and surround them with ice cubes. Sprinkle the tops of the custards with the turbinado sugar. Place under the hot grill until the sugar melts and turns golden brown. Alternatively, use a crème brûlée torch to caramelize the sugar.

Serves 4

coconut and ginger
crème brûlée

cardamom kulfi

6 cups milk
15 cardamom pods
$1/2$ cup superfine sugar

$1/2$ teaspoon lime zest, finely grated
$1/4$ cup pistachios, lightly toasted and coarsely chopped

Put the milk and 9 cardamom pods in a large, heavy-bottom saucepan. Bring to a boil, then reduce the heat and simmer for 15–20 minutes or until reduced by one-third. Strain into a freezable container. Add the sugar and stir until dissolved. Stir in the zest and half the pistachios. (Store the remaining nuts in an airtight container.) Cool for 30 minutes, then freeze until almost firm, stirring every 30 minutes—this can take 3–6 hours.

Rinse eight $2/3$-cup metal molds with cold water and shake out the excess. Pack the kulfi into the molds and freeze until completely firm. Remove the molds from the freezer 5 minutes before serving. Turn the kulfi out onto serving plates and sprinkle the reserved pistachios over the top. Lightly crush the remaining cardamom pods to release some of the seeds. Sprinkle a few seeds on top of the kulfi and sprinkle the pods around the base for decoration.

Serves 8

lemon and honey ricotta cake

4 cups ricotta cheese (see note)
1/2 cup honey
1 1/2 teaspoons pure vanilla
    extract
1/4 cup lemon juice
zest of 2 lemons, finely grated

1/2 teaspoon ground cinnamon
4 eggs, lightly beaten
1/4 cup all-purpose flour
poached nectarines or peaches,
    to serve (optional)

Preheat the oven to 325°F. Lightly grease and flour a 7-inch round springform cake pan.

Drain the ricotta if necessary, then process in a food processor until smooth. Add the honey, vanilla, lemon juice, zest, cinnamon, and eggs. Process until well combined. Add the flour and process until smooth.

Spoon the mixture into the prepared pan and bake for 1 hour or until light golden and still slightly soft in the middle. Turn the oven off, open the door slightly, and cool the cake in the oven. Put in the refrigerator to chill, then remove the cake from the pan. Serve at room temperature with poached fruit such as peaches or nectarines, if desired.

Note: Buy fresh ricotta sold in bulk at delicatessens and cheese stores. It has a much better texture and flavor than the prepackaged type.

Serves 10–12

Ginger adds a spicy warmth to both the crust and filling
of this rich cheesecake accompanied with sweet poached fruit.

preserved ginger cheesecake
with sauternes-poached plums

4 1/2 ounces ginger snaps
(15 cookies)

2 tablespoons unsalted butter,
melted

2 teaspoons powdered gelatin

2 cups cream cheese

14-ounce can sweetened
condensed milk

2 pieces preserved ginger in
syrup, finely chopped, plus
1/4 cup syrup (see note)

6 fresh plums

1/2 cup Sauternes

2 tablespoons superfine sugar

Put the ginger snaps in a food processor and process to fine crumbs (you should end up with 1 cup crumbs). Transfer the crumbs to a bowl and combine with the melted butter. Spoon the mixture into the bottom of an 8-inch round springform cake pan, pressing firmly. Refrigerate for 30 minutes.

Dissolve the gelatin in 1/4 cup boiling water. In a food processor, process the cream cheese, condensed milk, ginger, ginger syrup, and gelatin mixture until smooth. Pour over the chilled crust and refrigerate for 3 hours.

Halve or quarter the plums, depending on their size, and remove the pits. Combine the Sauternes and sugar in a saucepan and add the plums in a single layer. Gently poach the plums for 2 minutes on each side, then set aside to cool in the poaching liquid.

Arrange the plums, cut side up, on top of the cheesecake and drizzle with the poaching liquid.

Note: If you can't find preserved ginger in syrup, combine 6–7 finely chopped pieces of candied ginger with 1/4 cup water and 2 tablespoons sugar in a small saucepan. Bring to a boil, then boil for a few minutes until slightly reduced, syrupy, and infused with the ginger flavor. Cool, then use as directed in the recipe.

Serves 8

preserved ginger cheesecake with
sauternes-poached plums

almond vanilla cream torte

pastry cream
2/3 cup superfine sugar
5 egg yolks
1/4 cup all-purpose flour
2 cups milk
1 teaspoon pure vanilla extract

pastry
1/2 cup butter, softened
41/2 ounces superfine sugar
2 eggs, lightly beaten
31/2 cups all-purpose flour
1 teaspoon baking powder

1 egg yolk, beaten
heaping 1/3 cup flaked almonds
confectioners' sugar, to dust
ice cream or crème fraîche,
    to serve

For the pastry cream, beat the sugar and egg yolks together using electric beaters until very pale and creamy. Sift the flour in and lightly fold it through. Put the milk in a medium saucepan and bring to a boil. Remove from the heat and stir in the egg mixture. Stirring constantly, cook over low heat until smooth and thickened, 6–7 minutes. Stir in the vanilla and a pinch of salt.

For the pastry, put the butter and sugar in a bowl and beat with a wooden spoon until smooth. Beat in the eggs. Sift in the flour and baking powder and mix until uniform. Transfer the dough to a lightly floured surface and knead until smooth.

Preheat the oven to 350°F and put a cookie sheet on the center rack. Grease a 10-inch round fluted pie pan. Halve the dough. It will be soft, so roll each portion out to a 10$\frac{1}{2}$-inch circle on a large sheet of parchment paper or plastic wrap to enable an easy transfer to the pan. Use one circle of dough to line the bottom of the prepared pan, running the slight overlap up the sides of the pan. Cover with the pastry cream, spreading it in an even layer. Cover with the second circle of dough, pressing the edges together well to seal and also pressing the pastry into the flutes of the pan.

Brush the surface lightly with egg yolk and sprinkle with the almonds. Bake until cooked through and golden, about 35 minutes. Allow to cool, then dust with confectioners' sugar before serving. Serve with ice cream or crème fraîche.

Serves 8

coconut bavarian cream with papaya, pineapple, and lychee

1 1/4 cup dried, grated coconut
2 cups milk
1/3 cup palm sugar, grated, or light brown sugar, firmly packed
4 egg yolks
1 1/2 teaspoons powdered gelatin
1 cup whipping cream

1/2 small red papaya, seeded and peeled
1/2 small pineapple, peeled and cored
6 lychees or rambutans, peeled
1 tablespoon lime juice
pulp of 2 passion fruit
1–2 teaspoons superfine sugar, to taste

Spread the coconut over the bottom of a large frying pan. Stirring constantly, cook over low heat until lightly browned. Heat the milk in a medium saucepan until hot but not boiling. Turn off the heat and stir in the coconut. Set aside for 30 minutes for the flavor to infuse.

Put the palm sugar and egg yolks in a medium bowl and whisk together.

Strain the milk mixture, squeezing dry the coconut to extract all the liquid. Discard the coconut. Measure 1 1/4 cups of the milk and whisk this into the egg and palm sugar (discard any leftover milk). Return the mixture to the clean saucepan and whisk constantly over low heat until the custard thickens and coats the back of a metal spoon. Take care not to boil the custard. Remove from the heat.

Put the gelatin in a small bowl. Soften with 1 tablespoon water, then set it over a bowl of hot water to dissolve the gelatin. Whisk the mixture into the warm custard. Put the custard over a bowl of cold water and ice cubes and stir until the mixture cools and begins to set.

Meanwhile, whip the cream to firm peaks and fold into the custard mixture until smooth. Pour into four 3/4-cup metal or ceramic molds. Put on a tray, cover, and refrigerate for at least 6 hours or overnight to set.

Cut the papaya and pineapple into chunks. Halve the lychees or rambutans and remove the pits. Sprinkle the fruit with lime juice. Strain most of the seeds from the passion fruit pulp (leaving some seeds for decoration) and sweeten the juice with superfine sugar to taste.

To serve, briefly dip the molds into hot water and loosen the edges with a small knife. Turn out onto serving plates. Arrange the fruit pieces on the plates and drizzle over the passion fruit juice.

Serves 4

coconut bavarian cream with papaya, pineapple, and lychee

meringue roulade with raspberries and almonds

5 egg whites
1¹/₄ cups superfine sugar
2 teaspoons white wine vinegar
2 teaspoons cornstarch
1 teaspoon pure vanilla extract

raspberry sauce
2³/₄ cups fresh raspberries (see
   note)

2–3 tablespoons confectioners'
   sugar
3–4 tablespoons kirsch or
   raspberry liqueur
1 cup whipping cream
2 tablespoons confectioners'
   sugar, plus extra to dust

¹/₂ cup toasted, flaked almonds

Preheat the oven to 315°F. Grease a 10 x 12-inch jelly roll pan and line with parchment paper. Beat the egg whites in a bowl using electric beaters until firm peaks form. Beating constantly, add the sugar in a slow steady stream, then continue to beat for an additional 5 minutes, until the meringue is glossy and very thick. Fold in the vinegar, cornstarch, and vanilla. Spoon into the prepared pan and spread evenly. Bake until risen and firm but not browned, 15–20 minutes. Remove from the oven and leave in the pan on a wire rack to cool.

For the raspberry sauce, put half the raspberries in a food processor, add confectioners' sugar and kirsch or liqueur to taste, and process until puréed. Press through a sieve and discard the seeds. Set aside.

Whip the cream and 2 tablespoons of confectioners' sugar until thick. Add the remaining raspberries and fold through.

Place a large sheet of parchment paper on a flat surface and dust liberally with the extra confectioners' sugar and the toasted almonds. Turn out the cooled meringue onto the parchment paper with a short end toward you. Carefully remove the parchment paper that was used to line the pan. Spread the cream and raspberries evenly over the meringue, leaving a 4-inch border on the back end. Roll up with the aid of the parchment paper, enclosing all the cream and berries. Trim the edges to neaten. Pile on any loose almonds and dust with more confectioners' sugar.

With the seam underneath, carefully lift onto a serving plate. Cover with plastic wrap and refrigerate for 1 hour. To serve, cut into thick slices and drizzle with the raspberry sauce.

Note: Use frozen raspberries if fresh are not available. Thaw in the refrigerator, then stir through the cream just before serving.

Serves 10

custard tarts with rhubarb

shortcrust pie pastry
3 1/3 cups all-purpose flour, sifted
1 1/3 cups confectioners' sugar, sifted
heaping 3/4 cup unsalted butter, chilled and chopped
2 egg yolks

filling
1 cup milk
1 cup whipping cream

1/2 teaspoon pure vanilla extract
4 eggs
2/3 cup superfine sugar

14 ounces rhubarb (about 3 medium stalks rhubarb), trimmed, then cut into 3-inch pieces
1/3 cup light brown sugar, firmly packed
1/2 teaspoon ground cinnamon
1 teaspoon lemon juice

Preheat the oven to 400°F. Lightly grease eight loose-bottom tartlet pans, 4 inches in diameter and 1 1/4 inches deep.

For the pastry, process the flour, confectioners' sugar, butter, and a pinch of salt in a food processor until the mixture resembles coarse bread crumbs. Combine the yolks and 2 tablespoons chilled water. Add to the flour mixture and process until a dough forms. If the dough is not coming together, add a little more water, 1 teaspoon at a time. Turn out onto a work surface. Using your hands, press the dough into a flat, round disk. Cover with plastic wrap and refrigerate for 30 minutes.

Roll out the pastry on a lightly floured work surface to $1/8$ inch thick. Cut into rounds to fit the bottom and sides of the pans. Gently press into the pans, trim, cover with plastic wrap, and refrigerate for 30 minutes.

Line each pastry shell with parchment paper and fill with pastry weights or uncooked rice. Bake for 15 minutes, then remove the paper and weights and bake for 7–8 minutes or until the pastry is golden. Reduce the heat to 315°F.

For the filling, heat the milk, cream, and vanilla in a saucepan until just boiling. Whisk the eggs and sugar together until thick and pale. Pour the milk mixture into the egg mixture, whisking well. Cool the custard, then strain into the tartlet shells and bake for 25–30 minutes or until the filling has just set. Remove from the oven.

Increase the heat to 350°F. Put the rhubarb, brown sugar, cinnamon, lemon juice, and 2 teaspoons water in a small baking dish. Toss to combine, then cover with foil and bake for 30 minutes. Remove the tartlets from the pans. Just before serving, spoon on the rhubarb and juices. Serve warm or at room temperature.

Note: Instead of making the pastry, you can use 4 sheets of prepackaged frozen pie pastry; thaw for 10 minutes before using.

Makes 8

custard tarts with rhubarb

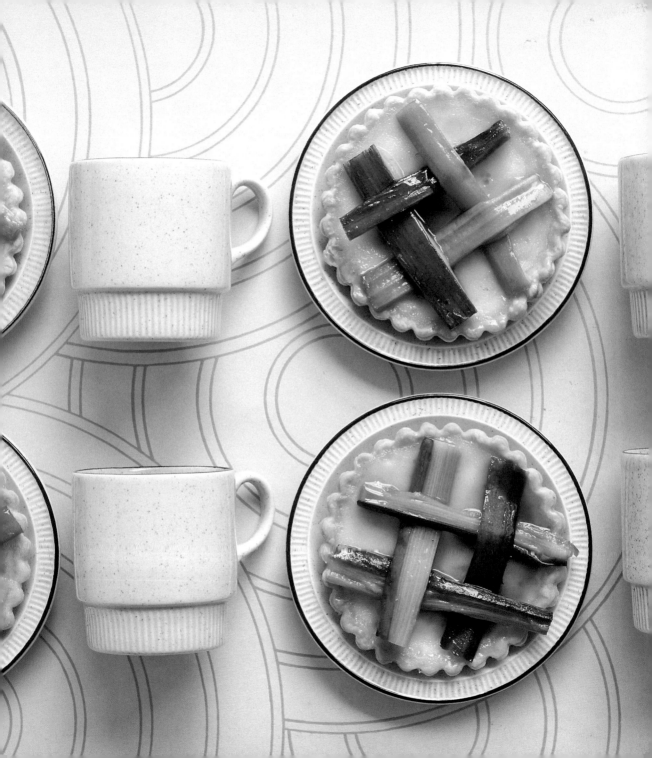

ricotta and cream cheese pudding

1 cup cream cheese
1/2 cup fresh ricotta cheese
1/2 cup superfine sugar
1/2 cup heavy cream
1 tablespoon honey, warmed
1 teaspoon pure vanilla extract
5 eggs, separated

1/4 cup golden raisins
3 1/4 cup toasted pistachios,
   chopped
grated zest and juice from
   1 lemon
fresh berries and whipping
   cream, to serve

Preheat the oven to 350°F. Grease an 8-cup ovenproof dish. In a large bowl, beat the cheeses and sugar with electric beaters until smooth. Beat the cream, honey, and vanilla well. Add the egg yolks one at a time, beating well after each addition. Stir in the raisins, nuts, lemon zest, and juice. Whisk the egg whites in a clean, dry bowl until stiff peaks form, then fold into the pudding mixture. Pour into the prepared dish. Put the dish in a large roasting pan and pour in enough hot water to come halfway up the sides of the dish. Cover the roasting pan with parchment paper, then tightly fold foil around the edges of the pan to seal. Bake 50–55 minutes, until the pudding is set, puffed, and firm. Serve with berries and cream.

Serves 6–8

gingersnap and lime cheesecake pots

6 gingersnaps
1/2 pint whipping cream
1 cup cream cheese, softened
2 eggs

1/3 cup superfine sugar
2 teaspoons lime zest, grated
4 tablespoons lime juice

Preheat the oven to 315°F. Place a gingersnap in the bottom of six 2/3-cup ramekins.

Combine the cream, cream cheese, eggs, sugar, lime zest, and juice in a food processor and blend until smooth. Pour the mixture over the cookies. Put the ramekins in a roasting pan and pour in enough water to come a third of the way up the sides of the ramekins. Bake for 50 minutes or until the mixture just firms in the center and begins to brown. Remove the cheesecakes from the roasting pan and cool to room temperature before serving in their ramekins.

Note: This dessert is best served without refrigeration, as this will keep the cookies crisp. However, if you need to cook the pots well in advance, they can be refrigerated then returned to room temperature before serving.

Makes 6

Kumquats, the smallest of the citrus family, add both sweet-tart piquancy and a jewel-like prettiness to this creamy dessert.

honey parfait with caramelized kumquats

1/4 cup honey
4 egg yolks, at room
    temperature
1/2 pint whipping cream,
    whipped to soft peaks

1 tablespoon orange liqueur,
    such as Grand Marnier
1 pound 2 ounces kumquats
    (about 40 kumquats)
1 1/2 cups superfine sugar

Put the honey in a small saucepan and bring to a boil. Beat the egg yolks in a bowl until thick and pale, then add the honey in a slow stream, beating constantly. Gently fold in the cream and liqueur. Pour the mixture into six 1/2-cup freezer-proof molds. Freeze for 4 hours or until firm.

Meanwhile, wash the kumquats well and prick the skins with a skewer. Place the kumquats in a large saucepan, cover with boiling water, and simmer for 20 minutes. Strain the kumquats and reserve 2 cups of the liquid. Return the liquid to the saucepan, add the sugar, and stir over medium heat until the sugar dissolves. Increase the heat and boil for 10 minutes. Add the kumquats and simmer for 20 minutes or until the kumquats are soft and the skins are smooth and shiny. Remove from the heat and set aside to cool. Using a slotted spoon, lift the kumquats out of the syrup. Reserve the syrup.

To serve, dip the molds in hot water for 5–10 seconds before inverting the parfait onto serving plates. Serve with the caramelized kumquats and a little of the syrup spooned over the top.

183

Serves 6

honey parfait with caramelized
kumquats

vanilla and cream cheesecakes

4 1/2 tablespoons unsalted
   butter, softened
1/2 cup superfine sugar
1 teaspoon lemon zest, finely
   grated
1 egg
1 egg yolk, extra
1/2 cup all-purpose flour
1 tablespoon self-rising flour
2 tablespoons sour cream

cheesecake topping

1 cup cream cheese, softened
1/2 cup superfine sugar
2 eggs
2/3 cup sour cream
1 vanilla bean or 1 teaspoon
   pure vanilla extract
2 tablespoons pine nuts

Preheat the oven to 350°F. Lightly grease twelve 1/2-cup friand or muffin pans and line the bottoms with parchment paper. Dust the sides of the pans with a little flour, shaking off any excess.

Using electric beaters, cream the butter, sugar, and zest in a bowl until pale and fluffy. Add the egg, then the egg yolk, beating well after each addition. Sift the flours into a bowl, then gently stir into the butter mixture alternately with the sour cream.

Divide the mixture among the prepared pans. Bake for 15 minutes or until a skewer inserted into the center of a cake comes out clean. Remove from the oven and allow to cool. Reduce the heat to 315°F.

For the cheesecake topping, beat the cream cheese and sugar in a small bowl until pale and fluffy. Add the eggs one at a time, beating well after each addition, then beat in the sour cream. If using the vanilla bean, split it down the middle and scrape out the seeds. Add the seeds (or vanilla extract) to the cheese mixture, mixing well. Spoon the topping evenly over the cooled cakes and sprinkle with the pine nuts.

Return to the oven and bake for 15 minutes or until the topping is just set. Remove from the oven, leave to cool slightly, then run a knife around the edge of each cake to loosen it. Turn out onto a wire rack and allow to cool. The cakes will keep for 3 days stored in an airtight container in the refrigerator.

Makes 12

Fragile-looking phyllo pastry is surprisingly hardy. As you work, cover the sheets with a clean damp cloth to keep them pliable.

vanilla custard log

3 cups milk
heaping 1/3 cup cornstarch
1 vanilla bean
6 egg yolks, at room
    temperature
2/3 cup superfine sugar
2 1/2 tablespoons orange zest,
    finely grated

8 sheets phyllo pastry
3 tablespoons ghee or unsalted
    butter, melted

confectioners' sugar, for dusting

Combine 1/4 cup of the milk with the cornstarch and mix to a paste. Put the remaining milk in a saucepan over medium heat. Split the vanilla bean lengthwise and scrape the seeds into the pan, discarding the pod. Add the cornstarch paste, egg yolks, sugar, and orange zest and whisk to combine. Stirring, boil for 4 minutes or until the custard is very thick. Remove from the heat, cover the surface with plastic wrap, and set aside to cool.

Preheat the oven to 350°F. Line a baking tray with parchment paper. Brush a sheet of phyllo pastry with the melted ghee or butter. Top with a second sheet of phyllo, brush with ghee or butter, then repeat with two more phyllo sheets. Make another stack of four sheets of pastry in the same way.

Spoon half the custard along the long edge of one rectangle of pastry, leaving a 3$\frac{1}{2}$-inch border, and shape into a 12-inch log. Carefully lift the border side of the pastry over the custard and roll up, tucking under the sides as you roll. Repeat with the remaining custard and pastry to make a second log.

Place the rolls on the prepared sheet and brush with melted ghee or butter. Bake for 20 minutes or until golden. Do not overcook the rolls or the custard will leak. Set aside to cool for 10 minutes. Dust with plenty of confectioners' sugar before serving.

Serves 8–10

fruity indulgences Versatile, colorful, and full of flavor, fruit is the dessert world's most reliable participant. From breakfast and brunch to lunch, afternoon tea, snack time, dinner, and

cocktail hour, the delicious goodness of fresh fruit is welcome at any occasion. And the good news for busy cooks: sometimes the simplest things are undoubtedly the best.

Bright berries; fragrant, tangy citrus; sweet, luscious pitted fruit; juicy, exuberant tropical fruit—for an everyday staple, fruit has a lot to offer. Be it a family lunch or when friends stay for dinner, if you have fruit in the fridge, sugar in the cupboard, and you can sneak some wine from the table, you can pretty much guarantee a tasty dessert. For this is surely one of the reasons why fruit has such enduring appeal: it requires very little effort to be transformed into a truly superb dessert. So although no one denies the value of the classic standby, the fruit platter, the recipes in this chapter demonstrate just how impressively easy it is to create something more spectacular. Fig and raspberry cake, Cointreau-glazed peaches, and mixed berry sundaes require neither unusual ingredients nor hours in the kitchen. What quickly becomes obvious is that when cleverly combined with flavors such as chocolate, wine, honey, caramel, or butterscotch, the humble apple, pliant peach, or everyday lemon becomes a bit of a wonder by the time it lands on the table. Depending on the fruit you have, you can create desserts that range in taste from tangy and cleansing to smooth and sweet, or rich and decadent. So can we be surprised to discover that after starting out as young children eating puréed apple and pear swirl, we eventually return not far from where we began, happily fighting over the last spoonful of mango fool or Eton mess? Fruit endures.

Named for the English college where it was created, this dessert
is simplicity itself, yet rich enough to satisfy any sweet tooth.

eton mess

4–6 large ready-made
   meringues
1²/₃ cups strawberries
   (see note)

1 teaspoon superfine sugar
1 cup heavy cream

Break the meringues into pieces. Cut the strawberries into quarters and
put them in a bowl with the sugar. Using a potato masher or the back of
a spoon, squash them slightly so they start to become juicy. Whip the
cream with a balloon or electric whisk until it is quite thick but not solid.
Gently mix everything together and spoon it into pretty serving glasses.
Serve immediately.

Note: Strawberries are traditionally used in this dish, but other berries may
be substituted. For a tropical version, use small chunks of mango, banana,
papaya, or pineapple, topped with fresh passion fruit pulp.

Serves 4

fig and raspberry cake

3/4 cup unsalted butter

heaping 3/4 cup superfine sugar,
    plus extra for sprinkling

1 egg, plus 1 egg yolk

2²/3 cups all-purpose flour

1 teaspoon baking powder

4 fresh figs, quartered

grated zest of 1 orange

1³/4 cups raspberries

Preheat the oven to 350°F. Lightly grease a 9-inch round springform cake pan. Cream the butter and sugar until pale. Add the egg and yolk and beat again. Sift in the flour, baking powder, and a pinch of salt. Combine to form a dough. Chill until firm.

Divide the dough in two and roll out one piece until large enough to cover the bottom of the pan. Transfer it to the prepared pan and set in place, pressing the dough up the sides a little. Cover with the figs, orange zest, and raspberries. Roll out the remaining dough and place it over the filling. Brush with water and sprinkle with a little sugar. Bake for 30 minutes, then serve warm.

Serves 6

Prescribed in medieval times as medicine, possets have now evolved into desserts—but they will still make you feel better.

lemon posset

½ cup superfine sugar
1¼ cups heavy cream
juice of 2 lemons (⅓ to ½ cup)

wafer cookies (or tuiles), to serve

Place the sugar and cream in a saucepan over low heat and bring to a boil slowly, stirring so the sugar dissolves and the cream does not boil over. Boil for 2–3 minutes, then add the lemon juice and mix well.

Pour the mixture into four ½-cup ramekins, cover with plastic wrap, and chill well for at least 2 hours or overnight. Serve with cookies such as wafers or tuiles.

Serves 4

peaches and raspberries cardinal

1 vanilla bean, split
1 cup superfine sugar
4 ripe peaches
1 pint fresh or thawed frozen
   raspberries
2 tablespoons confectioners'
   sugar

2–3 tablespoons Curaçao or
   other orange-based liqueur,
   to taste
vanilla, boysenberry, or
   raspberry ripple ice cream,
   to serve
1/4 cup shelled pistachios,
   toasted and coarsely chopped

Scrape the seeds from the vanilla bean. Put the seeds, the bean, superfine sugar, and 3 cups water in a large saucepan. Stir over low heat to dissolve the sugar. Bring to a boil, then reduce the heat to low and add the peaches. Simmer until tender, 4–6 minutes, depending on the ripeness of the fruit. Remove the peaches from the pan and slip off the skins when cool enough to handle. Let the syrup cool, then return the peaches to the syrup until ready to serve.

Reserve one-third of the raspberries. Purée the rest in a food processor with the confectioners' sugar and Curaçao. Strain the purée and discard the seeds. To serve, put a peach in a glass dish and coat with a little of the reserved cooking syrup. Add a scoop of ice cream, a drizzle of raspberry sauce, a few reserved raspberries, and a sprinkle of the pistachios.

Serves 4

peaches and raspberries
cardinal

The harmonious trio of meringue, cream, and berries has inspired many luscious desserts, such as this Australian classic.

classic pavlova

4 egg whites
1 cup superfine sugar
2 teaspoons cornstarch
1 teaspoon white vinegar
2 cups whipping cream

1^2/$_3$ cups strawberries, halved, to decorate
pulp of 3 passion fruit, to decorate

Preheat the oven to 315°F. Line a 13 x 11-inch cookie sheet with parchment paper.

Place the egg whites and a pinch of salt in a small, dry bowl. Using electric beaters, beat until stiff peaks form. Add the sugar gradually, beating constantly after each addition, until the mixture is thick and glossy and all the sugar has dissolved.

Using a metal spoon, fold in the cornstarch and vinegar. Spoon the mixture into a mound on the prepared sheet. Lightly flatten the top of the pavlova and smooth the sides. It should be circular and about 1 inch high. Bake for 1 hour or until pale cream and crisp. Remove from the oven while warm and carefully turn upside down onto a serving plate. Peel off the paper. Allow to cool, but do not refrigerate.

When ready to serve, lightly whip the cream until soft peaks form and spread it over the soft center of the pavlova. Decorate with the halved strawberries and pulp from the passion fruit. Cut into wedges to serve.

Note: While pavlovas are traditionally made with strawberries, other fresh berries may be used, or try banana slices and passion fruit pulp.

Serves 6–8

strawberries romanoff

5 cups strawberries, quartered
2 tablespoons Cointreau or
    other orange liqueur
1/4 teaspoon orange zest, finely
    grated

1 tablespoon superfine sugar
1/2 cup whipping cream
2 tablespoons confectioners'
    sugar

Combine the strawberries, liqueur, zest, and the superfine sugar in a large bowl. Cover and refrigerate for 1 hour. Drain the strawberries, reserving any juices. Purée about one-quarter of the berries with the reserved juices.

Divide the remaining berries among four pretty serving glasses. Beat the cream and confectioners' sugar until soft peaks form, then fold the berry purée through the whipped cream. Spoon the mixture over the top of the strawberries, then cover and refrigerate until required.

Serves 4

mango fool

2 very ripe mangoes
1/3 cup whipping cream

1 cup thick unsweetened yogurt

Take the flesh off the mangoes. The easiest way to do this is to slice down either side of the pit so you have two "cheeks." Make crisscross cuts through the mango flesh on each cheek, almost through to the skin, then turn each cheek inside out and slice the flesh from the skin into a bowl. Cut the rest of the flesh from the pit.

Purée the flesh using a food processor or blender. Whip the cream until soft peaks form.

Put a spoonful of mango purée in the bottom of four small glasses, bowls, or cups. Put a spoonful of yogurt on top and then repeat. When you have used up all the mango and yogurt, spoon one-quarter of the cream over each serving. Swirl the layers together just before you eat them.

Serves 4

mango fool

The sharpness of rhubarb makes a tangy counterpoint for tender, sweet cake in this recipe, suitable for an elegant afternoon tea.

rhubarb bars

10 1/2 ounces rhubarb (about 2 medium stalks rhubarb), trimmed and cut into 1/4-inch slices
1 1/2 cup superfine sugar
heaping 3/4 cup unsalted butter, chopped
1/2 teaspoon pure vanilla extract

3 eggs
3/4 cup all-purpose flour
3/4 teaspoon baking powder
1 tablespoon superfine sugar, extra
confectioners' sugar, for dusting
whipped or heavy cream, to serve

Combine the rhubarb and 1/2 cup sugar in a bowl. Set aside for 1 hour, stirring occasionally. When the rhubarb has released its juices and the sugar has dissolved, strain well and discard the liquid.

Preheat the oven to 350°F. Lightly grease an 8 x 12-inch rectangular shallow pan. Line the bottom with parchment paper, leaving the paper hanging over the two long sides for easy removal later.

Using electric beaters, cream the butter, 1 cup sugar, and vanilla in a bowl until pale and fluffy. Add the eggs one at a time, beating well after each addition. Sift the flour and baking powder over the mixture, then stir to combine. Spread the mixture evenly over the bottom of the prepared pan, then put the rhubarb over the top in a single layer. Sprinkle with the sugar.

Bake for 40–45 minutes or until golden. Leave to cool slightly in the pan, then carefully lift out, using the parchment paper as handles. Cut into 2-inch squares. Dust with confectioners' sugar and serve warm or at room temperature with whipped or heavy cream.

The rhubarb bars are best eaten on the day they are made.

Makes 24

In this Spanish-influenced recipe, sherry, orange, and spices flavor a smoky-sweet sauce to complement baked apples.

baked apples with pedro ximénez sauce

butter, for greasing
3 tablespoons golden raisins
1 cup Pedro Ximénez sherry (see note)
1 teaspoon orange zest, grated
2 tablespoons soft brown sugar
1/4 teaspoon ground cinnamon
31/2 tablespoons butter, softened
11/2 tablespoons slivered almonds, toasted

6 small red apples, with stalks attached
6 whole cloves
2/3 cup superfine sugar
1 strip orange zest, no pith
1/2 cinnamon stick
vanilla ice cream or whipped cream, to serve

Put the golden raisins in a small bowl with 1 tablespoon of the sherry and leave for 3–4 hours or overnight.

Preheat the oven to 350°F and liberally butter a shallow ovenproof dish. Mix the grated orange zest, brown sugar, cinnamon, and half the butter together until smooth. Stir in the raisins and almonds. Cut the top one-quarter off each apple and stick a clove into the outside of each top.

Cut out and discard the core, without cutting through the bottom of the apple. Fill the cavities with the raisin mixture and replace the apple tops. Put the apples in the prepared dish, sprinkle with 2 tablespoons of the raw superfine sugar, and put a little of the remaining butter on top of each apple. Pour water into the dish to a depth of 1/4 inch and bake until the apples are tender, 45–50 minutes.

Put the remaining raw superfine sugar, orange zest strip, cinnamon stick, and 1 1/2 cups water in a saucepan and stir over medium heat until the sugar dissolves. Bring to a boil, add the remaining sherry, and return to a boil. Reduce the heat to low and simmer until it thickens to a glossy syrup, 30–40 minutes. Strain into a small pitcher. Place the apples on serving plates, drizzle the warm syrup over them, and serve with vanilla ice cream or whipped cream.

Note: Pedro Ximénez is a sherry made from the grape variety of the same name. Any other good-quality sweet dark sherry may be substituted.

Serves 6

baked apples with pedro ximénez sauce

slow-baked quinces in honey

8 ripe quinces
1/4 cup unsalted butter, softened
1/4 cup honey

1/2 cup sweet white dessert
  wine, such as Sauternes
whipped cream or vanilla ice
  cream, to serve

Preheat the oven to 300°F.

Peel and halve the quinces. Don't worry about them discoloring, as they will turn very dark during cooking.

Use half the butter to grease a shallow ceramic dish large enough to take the halved quinces in one slightly overlapping layer.

Cut out and discard the cores of the quinces. Put the quinces, cut side up, in the prepared dish. Drizzle the honey on top and dot with the remaining butter. Pour the wine over the fruit. Cover with foil and bake for 2 hours, then turn the quinces over and return to the oven for another 2 hours. The quinces will turn a rich maroon red and the juices will caramelize. Serve hot with whipped cream or softened vanilla ice cream.

Serves 8

cointreau-glazed peaches

6 firm ripe peaches
I–2 tablespoons soft brown
   sugar
1/3 cup Cointreau

1 cup mascarpone cheese
ground nutmeg, to dust

Line a broiler pan with foil and lightly grease the foil. Preheat the broiler to medium. Cut the peaches in half, remove the pits, and place the peaches cut side up on the pan. Sprinkle the peaches with the sugar and Cointreau and broil for 5–8 minutes or until the peaches soften and a golden glaze forms on top.

Serve immediately with scoops of mascarpone. Dust lightly with nutmeg.

Serves 6

pink grapefruit meringue tartlets

1 quantity sweet pie pastry
    (page 176), or 4 prepackaged
    pastry sheets

grapefruit filling
7 tablespoons butter, chopped
6 eggs, lightly beaten
1 cup pink or ruby grapefruit
    juice
1 tablespoon ruby grapefruit
    zest, finely grated
3/4 cup superfine sugar

meringue
4 egg whites, at room
    temperature
1/2 cup superfine sugar
1 tablespoon cornstarch

Preheat the oven to 350°F. Lightly grease eight loose-bottom tartlet pans, 4 inches in diameter and 1 1/4 inches deep.

Roll out the pastry on a lightly floured work surface to 1/8 inch thick. Cut the pastry into 6 1/2-inch rounds to fit the base and sides of the pans. Gently press the sides to fit, trim the edges, then wrap the pans in plastic wrap and refrigerate for 30 minutes.

Line each pastry shell with parchment paper and fill with pastry weights or uncooked rice. Bake the pastry for 10 minutes, then remove the paper and weights and bake for 5 minutes or until golden. Allow to cool.

For the grapefruit filling, combine the butter, eggs, grapefruit juice, zest, and sugar in a heatproof bowl. Place over a saucepan of simmering water and whisk constantly for 10–15 minutes or until the mixture thickens. Set aside to cool. Spoon the cooled mixture into the pastry shells, smoothing the top. Place in the refrigerator for 30 minutes or until completely cold.

For the meringue, whisk the egg whites in a clean, dry bowl until soft peaks form. Add the sugar 1 tablespoon at a time, whisking well after each addition. Continue whisking until the mixture is stiff and glossy and the sugar has dissolved. Add the cornstarch and mix well. Spoon the mixture into a pastry bag fitted with a 3/4-inch plain tip. Remove the tartlets from the refrigerator and pipe the meringue over the top. Bake for 10 minutes or until the meringue is golden.

Makes 8

pink grapefruit meringue tartlets

baked passion fruit cheesecake

1/2 cup all-purpose flour
1/4 cup self-rising flour
31/2 tablespoons unsalted butter
2 tablespoons superfine sugar
grated zest of 1 lemon
2 tablespoons lemon juice

filling
21/3 cups cream cheese,
    softened
3/4 cup superfine sugar
1/4 cup all-purpose flour
1/2 cup strained passion fruit
    juice (see note)
4 eggs
2/3 cup whipping cream

Combine the flours, butter, sugar, and lemon zest in a food processor. Add the lemon juice and, using the pulse button, process until a dough forms. Cover with plastic wrap and refrigerate for 1 hour.

Preheat the oven to 350°F. Grease a 8-inch round springform cake pan.

Roll out the pastry to 1/4 inch thick. Roll the pastry around the rolling pin. Lift and ease it into the pan, pressing to fit, then trim the edges. Chill for 10 minutes. Bake for 15–20 minutes or until golden. Remove from the oven and cool. Reduce the heat to 300°F.

For the filling, use electric beaters to beat the cream cheese and sugar until smooth. Add the flour and passion fruit juice and beat until combined. Add the eggs one at a time, beating well after each addition. Stir in the cream, then pour the mixture over the cooled crust. Bake for 1 hour or until the center is just firm to the touch (move the cheesecake to the lowest shelf of the oven for the last 10 minutes of cooking; if necessary, cover with foil to prevent overbrowning). Cool the cheesecake in the pan before removing and serving in slices.

Note: You will need about 6 passion fruit to obtain $1/2$ cup passion fruit juice. Canned passion fruit pulp is not an adequate substitute. To assist in extracting the juice, it helps to blend the pulp, seeds and all, in a blender or food processor for a minute or two before straining it through a nonmetallic sieve.

Serves 6–8

toffee-glazed poached pears with caramel sauce

4 firm pears
1 cinnamon stick
heaping 3/4 cup superfine sugar
3 tablespoons shelled pistachios,
    finely chopped

caramel sauce
1/2 cup light brown sugar, firmly
    packed
1/3 cup butter, cubed

3/4 cup whipping cream
1 teaspoon pure vanilla extract

toffee
1 2/3 cups granulated sugar

whipped or heavy cream, to
    serve

Peel the pears, leaving the stems intact. Put the cinnamon stick, sugar, and 2 cups water in a medium saucepan. Stir over low heat to dissolve the sugar. Bring to a boil, add the pears, cover, then lower the heat and simmer until tender, 10–12 minutes. Turn with a slotted spoon halfway through cooking. Use the slotted spoon to carefully remove pears from the syrup, then cool to room temperature.

For the caramel sauce, put the sugar, butter, and cream in a small saucepan and stir over low heat until the butter has melted. Bring to a boil, then reduce the heat and simmer for 2 minutes. Remove from the heat, add the vanilla, and set aside until ready to use.

For the toffee, mix the sugar with $3/4$ cup water in a medium saucepan. Stir over low heat until the sugar dissolves. Bring to a rapid boil and cook without stirring until light golden brown, about 10 minutes.

Line two cookie sheets with parchment paper.

Quickly dip the cooled pears into the toffee, tipping the pan to achieve an even coating. The pears can be double-dipped for an extra thick layer. Working quickly, dip one side of each pear into the pistachio nuts. Put on one of the prepared sheets and leave to set.

Using a fork, drizzle the leftover toffee in a crisscross pattern onto the other prepared sheet. Leave to set, then break up into shards for serving.

To serve, put the pears on serving plates, surround with some caramel sauce, and stand a piece of toffee by the fruit. Serve immediately with a small bowl of whipped or heavy cream if desired.

Note: The pears should be eaten soon after being made, otherwise the moisture from their flesh will soften the toffee.

Serves 4

toffee-glazed poached pears with
caramel sauce

citrus delicious

4 1/2 tablespoons unsalted
   butter, softened
3/4 cups superfine sugar
3 eggs, separated
1/2 cup citrus juice (see note)

1 cup milk
1/2 cup self-rising flour
2 tablespoons citrus zest, finely
   grated (see note)
ice cream, to serve

Preheat the oven to 350°F. Grease a 5-cup ovenproof dish. Using electric beaters, cream the butter and sugar in a bowl until pale and fluffy. Add the egg yolks one at a time, beating well after each addition. Stir in the citrus juice, milk, flour, and zest, combining well.

Whisk the egg whites in a clean, dry bowl until stiff peaks form, then gently fold into the batter. Spoon the mixture into the dish. Put the dish in a large roasting pan and pour in enough hot water to come halfway up the side of the dish. Bake for 40–45 minutes or until golden and puffed (cover with foil if the top starts to brown too quickly). Serve hot or warm with ice cream.

Note: Use a mixture of oranges, lemons, and limes for the juice and zest.

Serves 4–6

poached vanilla peaches with raspberry purée and passion fruit sauce

1 1/2 cups superfine sugar
1 vanilla bean, halved lengthwise
4 peaches
heaping 3/4 cup fresh or thawed frozen raspberries

4 small scoops vanilla ice cream

passion fruit sauce
1/4 cup fresh passion fruit pulp
2 tablespoons superfine sugar

Put the sugar, vanilla bean, and 2 1/2 cups water in a large saucepan. Stir over low heat until the sugar dissolves. Bring to a slow boil, then add the peaches and simmer for 5 minutes or until just tender. Cool the peaches in the syrup, then remove with a slotted spoon. Peel and halve the peaches, removing the pits.

Put the raspberries in a food processor and process until puréed. Push the raspberries through a sieve, discarding the pulp. For the passion fruit sauce, stir together the passion fruit pulp and sugar until the sugar dissolves. To serve, divide the raspberry purée among 4 glasses. Arrange a scoop of ice cream and two peach halves on top. Spoon over the passion fruit sauce and serve immediately.

Serves 4

strawberry almond torte

crust
5 tablespoons butter, softened
1/4 cup superfine sugar
1 teaspoon lemon zest, grated
1/2 teaspoon pure vanilla extract
1 tablespoon strawberry liqueur
1 egg
1 egg yolk, extra
2/3 cup ground almonds
1 1/2 tablespoons all-purpose
   flour

filling
1 cup mascarpone cheese,
   softened
2 teaspoons confectioners' sugar
1 1/4 ounces almond biscotti,
   crushed (about 10 biscotti; to
   yield 1/3 cup when crushed)
1 teaspoon strawberry liqueur
1–2 tablespoons whipping cream
3 1/3 cups small strawberries,
   hulled
small mint leaves, to garnish
   (optional)
3 tablespoons strawberry jam,
   to glaze

Preheat the oven to 350°F and grease a 9-inch springform cake pan. Using electric beaters, beat the butter and sugar together until light and fluffy. Add the lemon zest, vanilla, strawberry liqueur, egg, and egg yolk and mix until combined. Fold in the ground almonds and flour. Spoon the mixture into the prepared pan and level the top with the back of a spoon. Bake until set, 15–20 minutes. Allow to cool in the pan for 5–10 minutes, then remove from the pan and transfer to a cake rack to cool completely. Meanwhile, mix the mascarpone, confectioners' sugar, crushed biscotti, and strawberry liqueur together until smooth, then gently stir in enough cream to give a spreadable consistency. The amount will depend on the thickness of the mascarpone. (Do not beat it in, as this may cause the mascarpone to split.)

Spread the mascarpone mixture over the top of the cake. Arrange the strawberries on top. Sprinkle the mint leaves around, if using.

Put the jam in a small saucepan with 2 tablespoons water. Heat gently until the jam melts, then strain it. Brush lightly over the strawberries and allow the glaze to cool before serving.

Serves 6

strawberry almond torte

raspberry soufflé

crème pâtissière
3 egg yolks
1 heaping cup superfine sugar
5 teaspoons cornstarch
1¹/2 teaspoons all-purpose flour
1 cup milk
¹/2 vanilla bean
2 teaspoons butter
2¹/2 tablespoons unsalted butter,
    softened

soufflé
3¹/4 cups fresh or thawed frozen
    raspberries
3 tablespoons superfine sugar
8 egg whites
confectioners' sugar, to dust

For the crème pâtissière, whisk together the egg yolks and 2 tablespoons of the sugar until pale and creamy. Sift in the cornstarch and flour and mix together well. Put the milk, 2 more tablespoons sugar, and vanilla bean in a saucepan. Bring just to a boil, then strain over the egg yolk mixture, stirring continuously. Pour back into a clean saucepan and bring to a boil, stirring constantly—it will be lumpy at first but will become smooth as you stir. Boil for 2 minutes, then stir in the 2 teaspoons of butter and leave to cool. Transfer to a clean bowl, lay plastic wrap on the surface to prevent a skin from forming, and set aside until needed.

Brush the inside of a 6-cup soufflé dish with the softened butter. Pour in the remaining sugar, turn the dish around to coat thoroughly, and then tip out any excess sugar. Preheat the oven to 375°F and put a cookie sheet in the oven to heat up.

For the soufflé, warm the crème pâtissière in a bowl over a saucepan of simmering water, then remove from the heat. Put the raspberries and half the sugar in a blender or food processor and mix until puréed (or mix by hand). Pass through a fine nonmetallic sieve to get rid of the seeds. Add the crème pâtissière to the raspberries and whisk together.

Beat the egg whites in a clean, dry bowl until firm peaks form. Gradually whisk in the remaining sugar to make a stiff, glossy mixture. Whisk half the egg white into the raspberry mixture to loosen it and then fold in the remainder with a large metal spoon. Pour into the soufflé dish and run your thumb around the inside rim of the dish, about 3/4 inch into the soufflé mixture, to help the soufflé rise without sticking.

Put the dish on the hot cookie sheet and bake for 10–12 minutes or until the soufflé is well risen and wobbles slightly when tapped. Test with a skewer through a crack in the side of the soufflé—the skewer should come out clean or very slightly moist. Serve immediately, dusted with a little confectioners' sugar.

Serves 6

orange gelatin and lime bavarian cream slice

orange gelatin
1 tablespoon powdered gelatin
zest of 2 oranges, finely grated
1¹/₂ cups fresh orange juice,
    strained
¹/₄ cup superfine sugar
2 tablespoons Grand Marnier
    or other orange liqueur
    (optional)

lime bavarian cream
1¹/₂ cups milk
zest of 3 limes, finely grated
4 egg yolks
¹/₂ cup superfine sugar
¹/₂ cup fresh lime juice (about 5
    limes)
1 tablespoon powdered gelatin
1 cup whipping cream
8–10 ladyfingers (savoiardi)

Lightly grease a 4¹/₄ x 8¹/₂-inch loaf pan. Line two sheets of parchment paper that have been folded into triple thickness across the pan and along its length. Allow for plenty of overhang. Don't worry that the corners of the pan aren't lined; the paper will give the Bavarian cream a smooth surface and enable it to be lifted out easily. For the orange gelatin, mix the gelatin with 2 tablespoons cold water in a small bowl. Put over a bowl of hot water and stir until dissolved.

Put the zest, juice, sugar, and liqueur in a saucepan and stir over low heat until the sugar dissolves. Simmer for 1 minute. Stir in the gelatin, then remove from the heat and cool to room temperature. Pour into the prepared pan and refrigerate until set, about 2 hours.

For the lime Bavarian cream, heat the milk and zest in a saucepan until almost boiling. Use electric beaters to beat the egg yolks and sugar until pale and creamy. Strain the hot milk in, beating continuously, then stir in the juice.

Mix the gelatin with 2 tablespoons cold water in a small bowl. Put over a bowl of hot water and stir until dissolved. Put the bowl containing the egg yolk and lime juice mixture over a saucepan of simmering water. Stir continuously until the mixture thickens slightly, 15–20 minutes. Stir the gelatin in, then remove from the heat and cool to room temperature. Whip the cream until soft peaks form, then gently fold it into the gelatin mixture. Spoon this mixture over the set orange gelatin. Arrange the ladyfingers lengthwise on top, covering the Bavarian cream. Press them in gently. Refrigerate until firmly set, 2–3 hours.

To serve, invert onto a flat plate or board, then carefully peel the paper off. Serve cut into slices.

Serves 10

orange gelatin and lime bavarian cream slice

coconut, mango, and almond pie

pastry
1 2/3 cups all-purpose flour
1/4 cup superfine sugar
1/4 cup ground almonds
2/3 cup chilled unsalted butter, cubed
2 egg yolks, at room temperature
1–2 tablespoons iced water

filling
3/4 cup unsalted butter, softened
heaping 3/4 cup superfine sugar
2 eggs, at room temperature
2/3 cup ground almonds
1/2 cup all-purpose flour
1 cup grated coconut
2 tablespoons coconut cream
1 tablespoon coconut liqueur

1 ripe mango
1/2 cup flaked coconut
vanilla ice cream or whipped cream, to serve

To make the pastry, put the flour, sugar, ground almonds, and butter in a food processor. Process until the mixture resembles fine crumbs. Add the egg yolks and process until smooth. Add the water, 1/2 teaspoon at a time, until the dough clumps together in a ball. Flatten the dough to a rough rectangle, cover with plastic wrap, and refrigerate for 30 minutes.

Preheat the oven to 375°F. Grease a 7$^1/_2$ x 10$^3/_4$-inch loose-bottom pie pan.

To make the filling, cream the butter and sugar with electric beaters for about 3 minutes. Add the eggs, one at a time, beating well after each addition. Fold in the ground almonds, flour, and grated coconut. Lightly stir in the coconut cream and coconut liqueur.

Roll out the pastry on a sheet of parchment paper until large enough to cover the bottom and sides of the pan. Transfer the pastry to the pan and trim any excess. Line the pastry with a sheet of parchment paper and add pastry weights or uncooked rice. Bake for 10 minutes, remove the paper and weights, and bake for another 5 minutes. Reduce the heat to 325°F.

Cut the cheeks from the mango, peel them, and cut into $^1/_8$-inch-thick slices. Spread the filling in the pastry case and arrange the mango slices in two rows down the length of the filling. Sprinkle the flaked coconut over the top and press it into the exposed filling with your fingertips, giving an uneven surface. Bake for 30 minutes or until the coconut begins to brown, then cover loosely with foil. Bake for another 35 minutes or until the filling sets and the top is golden brown. Serve warm with vanilla ice cream or cold with lightly whipped cream.

Serves 6–8

Few fruits are so evocative of summer as fresh berries. Use whatever mixture you wish for this luscious chilled dessert.

mixed berry sundae with raspberry cream

1³/4 cups sugar
juice of 1 lemon
2 pounds 4 ounces mixed
   summer berries (such as
   raspberries, blueberries,
   loganberries, and
   strawberries)

raspberry cream
2 cups fresh raspberries
¹/2 cup confectioners' sugar
¹/2 cup whipping cream

extra fresh berries, to serve

Heat the sugar and 2 cups water in a saucepan over low heat until the sugar dissolves. Bring to a boil, then reduce the heat and simmer for 5 minutes. Cool, then stir in the lemon juice.

Put the syrup and mixed berries in a processor fitted with the metal blade and process for 20 seconds or until smooth. Working in batches, press the purée through a nonmetallic sieve into a wide, deep plastic container. Discard the contents of the sieve. Freeze the mixture for 1–2 hours or until ice crystals form around the edges. Using an immersion blender or regular blender, pulse to break up the ice crystals. Return to the freezer and repeat this process for 4–5 hours until the berry mixture resembles soft snow.

To make the raspberry cream, blend the raspberries and sugar in a small processor for 10 seconds or until smooth. Press through a fine nonmetallic sieve. Discard the contents of the sieve. Lightly whip the cream until it just holds its shape. Fold the cream into the raspberry purée.

Serve the frozen sundae mixture in chilled glasses with a spoonful of raspberry cream and some fresh berries.

Serves 10

mixed berry sundae with
raspberry cream

Comforting yet refreshing at the same time, this pudding is very simple to make. Be sure to use the best ricotta you can find.

lime and ricotta pudding

5 tablespoons unsalted butter, softened
1 1/2 cups superfine sugar
2 teaspoons lime zest, finely grated
3 eggs, at room temperature, separated

1 1/2 cups fresh ricotta cheese (see note)
1/4 cup self-rising flour
1/4 cup lime juice
2 teaspoons confectioners' sugar

Preheat the oven to 350°F. Grease a 6-cup ovenproof dish.

Using electric beaters, beat the butter and superfine sugar with half the lime zest for 30 seconds. Add the egg yolks, one at a time, beating well after each addition. Gradually add the ricotta alternately with the flour and beat until thick and smooth. Stir in the lime juice.

Whisk the egg whites until stiff peaks form and gently fold into the ricotta mixture in two batches. Pour the mixture into the prepared dish and place in a roasting pan. Pour enough hot water into the pan to come halfway up the sides of the dish. Bake for 1 hour or until the pudding sets.

Sift the confectioners' sugar over the warm pudding and sprinkle with the remaining lime zest. Serve warm.

Note: The quality of the ricotta is important—it should be crumbly, moist, and fresh-tasting, not bland and dull. Buy bulk ricotta from a deli counter or specialty cheese store instead of the prepackaged variety that is sold in supermarkets.

Serves 4

folded raspberry and blueberry tartlets

2 cups all-purpose flour
3/4 cup cold butter, cubed
2 tablespoons superfine sugar

1 cup fresh or frozen
   blueberries (see note)
1 1/4 cup fresh or frozen
   raspberries (see note)
scant 1/4 cup superfine sugar
1 tablespoon all-purpose flour

1 egg, separated
4 sugar cubes, coarsely crushed

heavy cream or ice cream,
   to serve

For the pastry, put the flour and butter in a food processor and process until fine and crumbly. Add the sugar and pulse briefly. Add 5 tablespoons cold water and pulse until the mixture just comes together. Turn out onto a flat surface and press into a smooth ball. Cover with plastic wrap and refrigerate for 30 minutes.

Preheat the oven to 415°F. Line a cookie sheet with parchment paper.

Just before assembling the tarts, put the fruit in a bowl and gently fold through the superfine sugar and flour.

On a lightly floured surface, roll the pastry out to a thickness of about 1/8 inch and cut out four 6-inch rounds (you may need to cut two or three rounds and then reroll the pastry before cutting the rest). Transfer to the cookie sheet.

Thin the egg yolk with 1 teaspoon water and brush over the pastry. Pile the combined fruit into the center, leaving a 1 1/4-inch border. Fold and pleat the pastry edge to encase the fruit. Brush the edges with lightly beaten egg white and sprinkle the crushed sugar cubes over.

Bake for 15 minutes, reduce the heat to 400°F, and bake until the pastry is golden brown and crisp, about 25 minutes. Serve warm with heavy cream or ice cream.

Note: If using frozen berries, spread them on a flat plate lined with paper towels and thaw in the refrigerator. Transfer them to the pastry with a slotted spoon to avoid excess liquid.

Makes 4

folded blueberry and raspberry tartlets

cardamom pear shortcake

2 cups (about 16) dried pears
1 tablespoon superfine sugar
1¼ cups unsalted butter,
    chopped
¾ cup soft brown sugar,
    lightly packed

⅓ cup superfine sugar
3 eggs
2¼ cups all-purpose flour
1 teaspoon baking powder
1 teaspoon ground cardamom
confectioners' sugar, for dusting

Put the dried pears in a bowl, cover with boiling water, and soak for several hours or until the pears soften a little and the water cools.

Preheat the oven to 350°F. Lightly grease a 8 x 12-inch rectangular shallow pan with butter and line with parchment paper, extending the paper to hang over the two long sides.

Drain the water from the pears, reserving ½ cup. Put the pears, sugar, and reserved soaking water in a saucepan. Stir to dissolve the sugar. Bring to a boil, then reduce the heat and simmer covered for 5 minutes or until the pears are soft.

Using electric beaters, cream the butter and sugars in a bowl until pale and fluffy. Add the eggs one at a time, beating well after each addition. Sift together the flour, baking powder, and cardamom. Using a large metal spoon, fold the flour mixture into the butter mixture until well combined. Spread half the mixture evenly over the bottom of the prepared pan. Arrange the pears over it, then dot the remaining mixture over the pears to cover.

Bake for 40–45 minutes or until golden and a skewer inserted into the center of the cake comes out clean. Leave to cool in the pan, then carefully lift out, using the parchment paper as handles. Dust with confectioners' sugar and cut into 4 x 1$1/4$-inch fingers.

The cardamom pear shortcake will keep, stored in an airtight container in a cool place, for up to 3 days.

Makes 20

Can't decide between a fruit crisp and a pie? Try this recipe, a delicious mélange of the two.

caramelized peach and passion fruit crisp pie

1 large sheet frozen
   prepackaged pie pastry
   (see note)
2/3 cup all-purpose flour
1/4 cup soft brown sugar,
   lightly packed
41/2 tablespoons unsalted
   butter, chilled and cubed
1/4 cup dried, grated coconut

2 tablespoons hazelnuts,
   chopped, toasted, and
   skinned (see note, page 41)
4 peaches, peeled and sliced
1/3 cup superfine sugar
pulp of 3 passion fruit

Preheat the oven to 400°F. Roll out the pastry until it is large enough to cover the bottom and sides of a flan pan 8 inches across and 1 1/2 inches deep. Place the pastry in the pan and prick the bottom. Line the pastry shell with a sheet of parchment paper and add pastry weights or uncooked rice. Bake for 15 minutes, then remove the paper and weights and return to the oven for another 6–8 minutes. Remove from the oven and set aside to cool. Reduce the heat to 350°F.

For the topping, use your fingertips to rub the flour, brown sugar, and butter together. Add the coconut and chopped hazelnuts. Set aside.

Heat a frying pan over high heat. Toss the peach slices in the superfine sugar. Pour the peaches into the frying pan and cook, moving them occasionally until they are evenly coated in caramel. Add the passion fruit pulp and remove the pan from the heat.

Spoon the peach mixture into the pastry case and top with the crisp mixture. Bake for 20–25 minutes or until the top is golden brown.

Note: Choose a good-quality buttery pastry and let it set for 20 minutes before rolling out or it will crack and be difficult to work with.

Serves 6

caramelized peach and passion fruit
crisp pie

fig shortcake

1 1/2 cups all-purpose flour
1/2 cup self-rising flour
2 teaspoons ground cinnamon
1 teaspoon ground ginger
1 teaspoon pumpkin pie spice
1/2 cup soft brown sugar,
   firmly packed
1/2 cup ground hazelnuts
9 tablespoons unsalted butter,
   chopped

1 egg, lightly beaten
1 cup fig jam
2/3 cup hazelnuts, skinned,
   toasted, and finely chopped
   (see note, page 41)
confectioners' sugar, for dusting
   (optional)

whipped cream, to serve
   (optional)

Preheat the oven to 350°F. Lightly grease a 14 x 4 1/4-inch loose-bottom shallow pie pan.

Process the flours, spices, sugar, and ground hazelnuts in a food processor to just combine. Add the butter. Using the pulse button, process in short bursts until crumbly. Add the egg a little at a time, until the mixture comes together; you may not need all the egg. Divide the dough in half, wrap separately in plastic wrap, and refrigerate for 30 minutes.

Remove one ball of dough from the refrigerator and roll out between two sheets of parchment paper until large enough to fit the bottom and sides of the pan. Line the prepared pan, gently pressing the pastry to fit into the corners. Patch any holes with extra dough. Trim away the excess.

Spread the pastry with the fig jam. Coarsely grate the second chilled ball of dough into a bowl, add the chopped hazelnuts, and gently toss to combine. Press the mixture gently over the top of the jam, taking care to retain the grated texture. Bake for 35 minutes or until golden brown. Cool completely in the pan before cutting, and dust lightly with confectioners' sugar to serve. Serve with whipped cream if desired.

The shortcake will keep, stored in an airtight container, for up to 4 days or up to 3 months in the freezer.

Serves 12

Cherries are at their prime in midsummer. Celebrate their brief but glorious season with this rustic open pie.

free-form apple and cherry pie

1 1/2 tablespoons butter
3 green apples, peeled, cored, and cut into 1/2-inch pieces
1/3 cup soft brown sugar, lightly packed
1/2 teaspoon ground cinnamon
1/2 teaspoon ground ginger
1/2 teaspoon lemon juice
2 tablespoons all-purpose flour

2 cups pitted fresh, thawed, frozen, or drained canned cherries
1 large sheet prepackaged sweet pie pastry
1 egg yolk
1 tablespoon milk
1/4 cup apricot jam

Preheat the oven to 350°F. Grease and flour a large cookie sheet or pizza pan.

Melt the butter in a saucepan over medium heat. Add the apples, brown sugar, spices, and lemon juice. Cook covered for 5 minutes or until the apples soften a little. Remove from the heat and cool a little, then stir in the flour and cherries. Cool before filling the pastry.

Trim the pastry to make a circle and place it onto the prepared sheet. Pile the apple and cherry filling into the center of the pastry, leaving a 2-inch border. Fold the pastry over the filling, leaving the center uncovered and pleating the pastry to fit. Combine the egg yolk and milk to make a glaze and brush it over the edges of the pastry. Bake the pie on the bottom shelf of the oven for 35–40 minutes or until golden.

To make a jam glaze, combine the apricot jam and 1 1/2 tablespoons water in a small saucepan and bring to a simmer, stirring to combine. Brush the glaze over the pastry and fruit. Let the pie cool slightly before serving.

Serves 8

free-form apple and
cherry pie

tarte tatin

1¹/2 cups all-purpose flour
scant ³/4 cup unsalted butter
heaping 1¹/3 cup confectioners'
  sugar

1 large egg, beaten
3 pounds 5 ounces dessert apples
³/4 cup superfine sugar
heavy cream, to serve

Sift the flour and a pinch of salt onto a work surface and make a well in the center. Put 7 tablespoons of the butter into the well. Using a pecking action with your fingertips and thumb, work the butter until it is very soft. Add the sugar to the butter and mix together. Add the egg to the butter and mix together.

Gradually incorporate the flour, flicking it onto the mixture and then chopping through it until you have a rough dough. Bring together with your hands and then knead a few times to make a smooth dough. Roll into a ball, wrap in plastic wrap, and refrigerate for at least 1 hour.

Peel and core the apples and cut them into quarters. Put the remaining butter and sugar in a deep 10-inch frying pan with an ovenproof handle. Heat until the butter and sugar have melted together. Arrange the apple quarters tightly, one by one, in the frying pan, making sure to leave no gaps. Remember that you will be turning the pie out the other way up, so arrange the apple pieces so that they are neat underneath.

Cook over low heat for 35–40 minutes or until the apples are soft, the caramel lightly browned, and any excess liquid evaporated. Baste the apples with a pastry brush every so often, so that the top is caramelized as well. Preheat the oven to 375°F.

Roll out the pastry on a lightly floured surface into a circle slightly larger than the frying pan. Lay the pastry over the apples in the pan and press down around the edges to enclose completely. Roughly trim the edge of the pastry and then fold the edge back on itself to finish neatly.

Bake for 25–30 minutes or until the pastry is golden and cooked. Remove from the oven and let rest for 5 minutes before turning out. (If any apples stick to the pan, just push them back into the hole in the pastry.) Serve with a dollop of heavy cream.

Serves 8

banana fritters with butterscotch sauce

butterscotch sauce
4¹/2 tablespoons unsalted butter
¹/3 cup dark corn syrup
¹/3 cup soft brown sugar,
　　lightly packed
¹/4 cup superfine sugar
²/3 cup whipping cream
¹/2 teaspoon pure vanilla extract

oil for deep-frying
4 firm bananas
confectioners' sugar, to dust
　　(optional)
ice cream, to serve

batter
1 cup self-rising flour
1 egg, beaten, at room
　　temperature
³/4 cup club soda
1¹/2 tablespoons unsalted
　　butter, melted

For the sauce, put the butter, corn syrup, brown sugar, and superfine sugar in a small saucepan. Stir over low heat for 2–3 minutes or until the sugar dissolves. Increase the heat and simmer for 3–5 minutes, taking care not to burn the sauce. Remove the pan from the heat and stir in the cream and vanilla.

For the batter, sift the flour into a bowl and make a well in the center. Add the egg and club soda, whisk until smooth, then whisk in the butter.

Fill a saucepan one-third full of oil and heat to 400°F or until a cube of bread dropped into the oil browns in 5 seconds.

Cut each banana lengthwise into halves and add to the batter in batches. Use a spoon to coat the banana in the batter.

Using a slotted spoon, carefully lower the bananas into the hot oil in batches. Fry each batch for 2–3 minutes, turning until the fritters are puffed and golden brown all over. Drain the fritters on paper towels. Serve the fritters hot, dusted with confectioners' sugar if desired. Accompany with ice cream and the butterscotch sauce.

Note: Any leftover sauce can be stored covered in the refrigerator for up to 2 weeks.

Serves 4

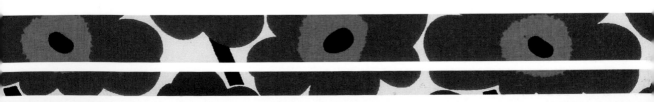

banana fritters with
butterscotch sauce

Most berries freeze wonderfully well, meaning that this luscious
"summer" dessert can be made all year round.

summer berry dessert

9 thin slices white bread, crusts
   removed (see notes)
2 1/2 cups mixed frozen berries
   (see notes)
2 cups fresh or frozen
   raspberries (see notes)

3/4–1 cup superfine sugar,
   to taste

heavy cream or mascarpone
   cheese, to serve

Cut a circle from one of the slices of bread to fit the bottom of a 4-cup bowl. Cut the remaining bread slices into angled pieces and fit them around the bowl, overlapping them as necessary. Reserve some bread for the top.

Put the berries in a large saucepan and gently stir in 3/4 cup of the sugar. Cover and simmer for 3–4 minutes, until the sugar dissolves and the berry juices begin to run. Taste for sweetness, adding some of the remaining sugar if needed.

Strain $1/2$ cup of the juice from the fruit and reserve. Spoon the fruit into the bread-lined bowl using a slotted spoon, reserving about $1/2$ cup of the juice. Pack it in well, then completely cover the top with the reserved bread slices. Put the bowl on a small cookie sheet. Cover the bowl with plastic wrap and put a flat plate on top to fit neatly inside the rim. Put 2 heavy cans (or similar) on top to act as weights. Refrigerate overnight.

Just prior to serving, invert the dessert onto a serving plate. Spoon over the reserved juice to soak any bread that has not colored. Serve cut into wedges with heavy cream or mascarpone.

Notes: For best results, use loaf bread thinly sliced rather than presliced bread. The latter doesn't absorb juices as well as loaf bread. Put the frozen berries on a flat tray lined with paper towels and thaw in the refrigerator.

Serves 6–8

Calvados, a French apple brandy aged in oak, is the foundation of a rich sauce for these poached apples.

glazed apples with calvados sauce

1 cup superfine sugar
1 strip lemon zest, no pith
1 tablespoon lemon juice
3 tablespoons Calvados
6 small to medium Golden
    Delicious apples

4$^{1}/_{2}$ tablespoons butter, cubed
mascarpone cheese, to serve
4 small fresh lemon leaves
    (optional)

Put the sugar, lemon zest, lemon juice, half the Calvados, and 2$^{1}/_{2}$ cups water into a saucepan large enough to hold the apples in a single layer. Stir to dissolve the sugar, then bring to a boil.

Peel the apples, leaving the stalks intact. Add them to the syrup and poach over low heat until tender, about 10–15 minutes, depending on the age of the apples. Carefully turn them once during cooking. Remove the apples once they are tender, put on serving plates, and set aside until ready to serve.

Add the butter and lemon leaves, if using, to the pan. Increase the heat and boil until the syrup thickens and darkens to a light caramel, 10 15 minutes. Stir in the remaining Calvados.

Baste the apples with the syrup (use a bulb baster if you have one, as it makes it easier to draw up the syrup without damaging the apples) and discard the lemon zest. Serve hot or cold with a dollop of mascarpone and the lemon leaves as garnish if desired.

Serves 6

glazed apples with calvados sauce

summer berries in champagne gelatin

4 cups champagne or sparkling white wine	4 strips lemon zest
2 tablespoons powdered gelatin	4 strips orange zest
heaping 1 cup sugar	$1^2/_3$ cups strawberries, hulled
	$1^2/_3$ cups blueberries

Pour half the champagne into a bowl and let the bubbles subside. Sprinkle the gelatin over the top in an even layer. Leave until the gelatin is spongy—do not stir. Pour the remaining champagne into a large saucepan, add the sugar and zests, and heat gently until all the sugar dissolves, stirring constantly. Remove the saucepan from the heat, add the gelatin mixture, and stir until thoroughly dissolved. Leave to cool completely, then remove the zest.

Divide the berries among $1/_2$-cup stemmed wine glasses and gently pour the gelatin over them. Refrigerate until set. Remove from the refrigerator 15 minutes before serving.

Serves 8

cherry clafoutis

3¹/3 cups unpitted cherries, stems removed
¹/2 cup all-purpose flour
heaping ¹/3 cup superfine sugar
2 eggs, lightly beaten, at room temperature
³/4 cup milk
1 teaspoon pure vanilla extract
1¹/2 tablespoons unsalted butter, melted
confectioners' sugar for dusting

Preheat the oven to 415°F. Lightly grease a 6-cup round ovenproof dish. Spread the cherries evenly over the bottom of the prepared dish.

Put the flour, superfine sugar, and a pinch of salt in a bowl and stir to combine. Add the eggs and beat well. Combine the milk, vanilla, and butter, then pour into the egg mixture and beat until combined.

Carefully pour the batter over the cherries and bake for 40 minutes or until the clafoutis is golden brown. Cool for at least 10 minutes, then serve warm or cold, dusted with confectioners' sugar.

Serves 8

ricotta cake with fruits of the forest

cake
3 eggs
3/4 cup superfine sugar
1 cup all-purpose flour
1 teaspoon baking powder
1 tablespoon vegetable oil
1/3 cup boiling water

1 3/4 cups mixed fresh berries
(see notes)
2 1/2 teaspoons powdered
gelatin
2 teaspoons strawberry liqueur
1/2 cup superfine sugar
2 teaspoons lemon juice

filling
2 cups ricotta cheese (see notes)
3/4 cup thick yogurt
1 1/4 cups confectioners' sugar
1 1/3 cups whipping cream
1 teaspoon pure vanilla extract

For the cake, preheat the oven to 350°F. Grease a 10-inch round springform pan and line the bottom with parchment paper.

Cream the eggs and sugar in a bowl for 3 minutes using electric beaters. Sift in the flour, baking powder, and a pinch of salt, then fold through. Add the oil and water and stir quickly until combined. Pour into the prepared pan and bake until set, about 20 minutes. Turn out and allow to cool completely on a wire rack.

For the filling, process the ricotta, yogurt, and confectioners' sugar in a food processor until smooth. Whip the cream in a large bowl until stiff peaks form. Fold the ricotta through. Carefully fold in 1/2 cup of the berries.

Using a long bread knife, carefully slice the cake in half through its middle. Put the lower half back into the bottom of the cleaned reassembled springform pan. Spoon the ricotta mixture on top, then cover with the top of the cake. Press down firmly to eliminate air pockets. Put the pan on a large plate to collect any juices draining from the ricotta and refrigerate while you prepare the remaining berries.

Mix the gelatin and liqueur together in a small bowl and put over a bowl of hot water. Stir until dissolved. Put the remaining berries, the superfine sugar, and lemon juice in a saucepan and cook over high heat until the sugar dissolves and the mixture is syrupy but whole pieces of berry remain, about 1–2 minutes. Strain, reserving 1/2 cup of syrup. Stir a spoonful or two of the reserved syrup into the gelatin mixture, then gently stir back into the fruit. Cool for 10 minutes, then refrigerate until partially set, about 30 minutes. Spread the berry syrup over the cake leaving about 1/3 inch around the edge uncovered. Refrigerate for 8 hours or overnight before serving.

Notes: Bulk ricotta from a deli counter is preferable to the prepacked type in tubs. Use any seasonal berries; only use strawberries if they are very small.

Serves 8

ricotta cake with fruits of the forest

blueberry semolina cakes

¹/₄ cup self-rising flour

¹/₃ cup semolina

1 cup superfine sugar

¹/₄ cup ground almonds

¹/₂ teaspoon lemon zest, finely grated

4 egg whites, lightly beaten

9 tablespoons unsalted butter, melted

¹/₂ cup blueberries

¹/₂ cup sliced almonds

confectioners' sugar, for dusting

Preheat the oven to 325°F. Line a 12-hole standard muffin pan with paper cupcake liners.

Sift the flour and semolina into a large bowl, add the sugar, ground almonds, and lemon zest. Stir to combine. Add the egg whites and beat the ingredients using electric beaters until combined. Pour in the melted butter and continue to beat until smooth and well combined. Add the blueberries and fold in to just combine, then spoon the batter into the paper liners. Sprinkle the sliced almonds over the batter and bake for 30 minutes or until a skewer inserted into the center of a cake comes out clean. Turn out onto a wire rack to cool. Dust with sifted confectioners' sugar to serve.

The blueberry cakes are best served on the day they are made.

Makes 12

peach galettes

1 quantity sweet pie pastry
   (page 176)
1 pound 5 ounces peaches,
   pitted and thinly sliced
1¹/₂ tablespoons butter, melted
1 tablespoon honey

1 tablespoon superfine sugar
¹/₄ teaspoon ground nutmeg
1 egg yolk
1 tablespoon milk
3 tablespoons apricot jam
¹/₄ cup sliced almonds, toasted

Lightly grease a cookie sheet or line it with parchment paper. Roll out the pastry on a lightly floured work surface to ¹/₈ inch thick. Cut out twelve 4¹/₂-inch rounds. Gently toss together the peach slices, butter, honey, sugar, and nutmeg in a bowl. Divide the peach mixture among the pastry rounds, leaving a ¹/₂-inch border. Fold the pastry over the filling, leaving the center uncovered, pleating the pastry at ¹/₂-inch intervals to fit. Place on the sheet and refrigerate for 30 minutes.

Meanwhile, preheat the oven to 400°F. Combine the egg yolk and milk in a small bowl and brush this glaze over the edges of the pastry. Bake for 30 minutes or until golden.

In a small saucepan, stir the jam and 1 tablespoon water over low heat until smooth. Brush the mixture over the hot galettes, then sprinkle with almonds. Cool before serving.

Makes 12

citrus custard cake with kiwifruit

cake
1 1/2 cups self-rising flour
1 teaspoon baking powder
3/4 cup butter, softened
3/4 cup superfine sugar
3 eggs
1/2 cup dried, grated coconut
zest of 1 lime, finely grated
1 tablespoon lime juice
2 tablespoons milk

white chocolate cream
2/3 cup white chocolate
1 cup whipping cream

citrus custard
3 tablespoons cornstarch
1/4 cup lime juice
1/4 cup lemon juice
1/4 cup orange juice
3/4 cup superfine sugar
3 egg yolks
1 1/2 tablespoons butter,
    softened

citrus syrup
1/2 cup superfine sugar
1 tablespoon lime juice
1 tablespoon orange juice

4 ripe kiwifruit
1/2 shredded or flaked coconut,
    toasted

Preheat the oven to 350°F. Grease two 8-inch shallow cake pans and line the bottoms with parchment paper. Sift the flour and baking powder into a medium bowl, add the butter, sugar, eggs, coconut, lime rind and juice, and milk. Beat with electric beaters for 1 minute until smooth and creamy.

Divide between the prepared pans and smooth the surface. Bake until firm and springy to touch, 20–25 minutes. Remove from the oven, leave for 5 minutes, then turn out onto wire racks to cool completely. With a serrated knife, cut each cake in half horizontally.

For the white chocolate cream, put the chocolate in a heatproof bowl. Heat the cream in a small saucepan until hot. Pour the cream over the chocolate and stir until the chocolate is melted. Refrigerate until cold, then beat with electric beaters until soft peaks form.

For the citrus custard, put the cornstarch, juices, sugar, egg yolks, and butter in a medium saucepan and whisk until smooth. Put over low heat and whisk until the mixture boils and thickens. Set aside to cool. For the citrus syrup, put the sugar, juices, and 3 tablespoons water in a small saucepan. Stir over medium heat to dissolve the sugar, then boil without stirring for 5 minutes, until a little syrupy. Brush all the cut surfaces of the cakes with the syrup. Peel and thinly slice the kiwifruit.

To assemble the cake, put one layer of cake on a serving plate. Spread with one-third of the citrus custard and arrange one-third of the kiwifruit slices on top. Continue this layering, ending with a cake layer on top. Spread the white chocolate cream all over the cake and sprinkle with toasted coconut.

Serves 10

alcoholic haze Normally when it comes to desserts, you think fruit, chocolate, cream, pastry—oh, and maybe a dash of alcohol would go nicely, too. This time it's the reverse: alcohol, in all its

myriad, heady, warming forms, is at the heart of these recipes. It's enough to make you pause for a fraction—just a fraction, mind—before turning the next page. Now, onward and indulge!

What goes with alcohol? A lot, it would seem. Fruit of every season, from summery berries to winter's pears and blood oranges; nuts such as chestnuts and almonds; chocolate (of course); flavorings like vanilla and coffee; and pastry and sweet breads such as pound cake and ladyfingers. You would be excused for thinking that just about any scrumptious dessert with a dash of alcohol could go in this chapter. Yet you would be wrong. For, it is the alcohol that defines these recipes; without it, they just wouldn't be the same. A trifle is not a trifle without a splash of sherry or Marsala, and what to do with sober crêpes? This is not a large chapter, which is perhaps a good thing, but each recipe is a pleasant voyage of discovery in the world of cooking with alcohol. Brandy, rum, whisky, red wine, cider, Kahlùa—all the old favorites are here, and a few more besides. With the well-chosen addition of alcohol, the flavor and aroma of a dish are unforgettably changed—desserts can become mellower and warmer, subtly sweet, or stronger and sharper. Many of the recipes in this chapter tread a simple path to your door, such as piña colada mousse or limoncello cream with tipsy ruby berries. A few recipes, however, go for gold: Grand Marnier soufflés with liqueur sabayon spring to mind. In all cases, the presence of alcohol makes these dishes what they are—very nice, indeed

apple cider dessert cake with cider sauce

cider sauce
4 cups sweet hard apple cider
1/4 cup bourbon
3 tablespoons dark corn syrup
2 tablespoons apple cider
    vinegar
1/3 cup dark brown sugar,
    lightly packed
1 cinnamon stick
1/2 teaspoon pure vanilla extract
1 cup whipping cream

cake
1/3 cup butter, softened
3/4 cup dark brown sugar,
    lightly packed

1 teaspoon pure vanilla extract
2 eggs
3/4 cup sweet hard apple cider
3 tablespoons vegetable oil
2 tablespoons bourbon
heaping 13/4 cups all-purpose
    flour
1 teaspoon baking powder
1/4 teaspoon baking soda
1 teaspoon salt

topping
3/4 cup whipping cream
3 tablespoons thick yogurt
1/4 teaspoon pure vanilla extract
1 teaspoon superfine sugar

For the sauce, put the cider, bourbon, corn syrup, vinegar, sugar, and cinnamon stick in a large saucepan and bring to a boil. Simmer over low heat for 10 minutes, then stir in the vanilla and cream. Increase the heat to medium and boil until reduced to about 1 cup, about 40 minutes, taking care that it does not burn. Discard the cinnamon stick.

For the cake, preheat the oven to 350°F. Grease an 8-inch springform cake pan and line the bottom with parchment paper. Flour the sides of the pan. In a large bowl, beat the butter until creamy using electric beaters. Add the sugar and vanilla and beat until smooth. Add the eggs one at a time, beating well after each addition.

Mix the cider, oil, and bourbon in a pouring bowl. Sift the flour, baking powder, baking soda, and salt into a bowl. Fold into the butter mixture in three batches, alternating with the cider mixture. Spoon two-thirds of the batter into the prepared pan. Using a spoon, carefully drizzle half of the cider sauce over the top. Gently spoon the remaining batter on top and spread it evenly, being careful not to mix the layers. Bake until a skewer inserted in the center comes out clean, about 45 minutes. Cool in the pan for 10 minutes, then turn out onto a wire rack. Cool for 15 minutes, then peel off the parchment paper. Cool for an additional 45 minutes.

For the topping, whip the cream, yogurt, and vanilla until soft peaks form. Gradually incorporate the superfine sugar and continue whipping until stiff. Spread the topping over the top of the cake and level the surface.

Reheat the remaining cider sauce. Slice the cake into wedges and serve warm or cold, with a little warm cider sauce drizzled over the top.

Serves 8

This English classic is the perfect canvas for rich and lavish decoration—go wild with cream, nuts, fruit, or grated chocolate.

trifle

2 cups raspberries
4 slices pound cake or one
 7-ounce jelly roll
3 tablespoons sweet sherry
 or Madeira
4 eggs
2 tablespoons superfine sugar

2 tablespoons all-purpose flour
2 cups milk
1/4 teaspoon pure vanilla extract
1 cup whipping cream
3 tablespoons sliced almonds,
 toasted, to decorate
1 1/2 cups raspberries, extra
 to serve (optional)

In a small bowl, crush some of the raspberries gently with the back of a spoon to release their tart flavor, leaving the rest whole. Put the cake in the bottom of a serving bowl, then sprinkle it with the sherry. Sprinkle half of the raspberries over the top.

Mix the eggs, sugar, and flour together in a bowl. Heat the milk in a pan until almost boiling, pour it over the egg mixture, stir well, and pour back into a clean pan. Cook over medium heat until the custard boils and thickens and coats the back of a spoon. Stir in the vanilla, cover the surface with plastic wrap, and leave to cool.

Pour the cooled custard over the raspberries and leave to set in the refrigerator—it will firm up but not become solid. Place the remaining raspberries on top. Whip the cream until soft peaks form and spoon it over the raspberries. Decorate with almonds and refrigerate for several hours before serving. Serve with extra raspberries if desired.

Serves 6

trifle

hot chocolate soufflé with brandy chocolate sauce

chocolate brandy sauce
2/3 cup dark chocolate, chopped
2 tablespoons butter, cubed
1/2 cup whipping cream
2 tablespoons confectioners'
　　sugar
2 tablespoons brandy

superfine sugar, to sprinkle

soufflé
1 cup dark chocolate, chopped
4 eggs, separated
1 teaspoon pure vanilla extract
2 egg whites, extra

confectioners' sugar,
　　to dust
whipping cream, to serve

For the chocolate brandy sauce, heat the chocolate and butter in a heatproof bowl over (not touching) a saucepan of simmering water until just melted and smooth, stirring often. Whisk in the cream, confectioners' sugar, and brandy. Set aside.

Preheat the oven to 400°F. Butter a 5-cup soufflé dish and sprinkle with superfine sugar. Tap out the excess. Fix a collar around the dish (see note).

For the soufflé, heat the chocolate in a heatproof bowl over (not touching) a saucepan of simmering water, stirring often, until just melted. Remove from the heat and whisk in the egg yolks and vanilla.

Put the six egg whites in a clean bowl. Beat with electric beaters until firm peaks form. Stir one-quarter of the egg white into the chocolate mixture with a large metal spoon, then gently fold in the remainder. Pour into the prepared dish. Put the dish on a cookie sheet and bake until puffed and firm to the touch, 20–25 minutes.

Gently reheat the chocolate sauce and pour it into a small pitcher.

Dust the soufflé with confectioners' sugar and serve at once with the sauce and cream.

Note: For the collar, cut a sheet of parchment paper long enough to wrap around the dish and fold it into thirds lengthwise. Grease the inner surface lightly. Wrap it around the dish so that it stands about 1 1/2 inches higher than the rim of the dish, and tie in position with jute or cotton string.

Serves 4

crêpes with passion fruit liqueur butter

crêpes
1 cup all-purpose flour
2 eggs, lightly beaten
1 cup milk
2 tablespoons butter, melted
1 teaspoon lime zest, grated
1 tablespoon Galliano liqueur

passion fruit liqueur butter
1/2 cup superfine sugar
1/2 cup strained passion fruit
   juice (see note)
1 teaspoon lime zest, grated
3 tablespoons Galliano liqueur

2 tablespoons butter, cubed
ice cream or whipping cream,
   to serve

Put the flour in a food processor and briefly process. With the motor running, pour in the eggs and one-quarter of the milk and process until incorporated. Add the remaining milk, the melted butter, lime zest, and liqueur. Process until smooth. Pour into a pitcher and set aside to thicken for 20 minutes.

Heat a lightly greased 6 1/2-inch crêpe pan. Pour in a thin layer of batter to cover the pan completely, then tip out any excess. Cook over medium heat until lightly golden and crisp around the edges, then flip and cook the other side. Transfer to a plate. Cook the remaining batter, stacking the

crêpes. You will need 12 crêpes, so there is enough batter for a couple of failures.

For the passion fruit liqueur butter, put the sugar and 3 tablespoons water in a large frying pan. Stir over moderate heat to dissolve the sugar. Increase the heat and boil without stirring until the sugar evenly caramelizes to a rich dark color, 3–4 minutes. Lower the heat, then carefully and slowly pour on the passion fruit juice, taking care that it does not splatter and burn you. Stirring, cook over low heat until the caramel dissolves. Stir in the grated lime zest and liqueur.

Fold each of the 12 crêpes into quarters and arrange them overlapping in the sauce. Dot with the diced butter. Over low heat, gently shake the pan and spoon the sauce over the crêpes until the butter melts and mixes into the sauce. Serve 3 per person, with ice cream or whipping cream.

Note: You will need the pulp of about 9 passion fruit, sieved, to yield $1/2$ cup of juice.

Serves 4

crêpes with passion fruit
liqueur butter

chocolate rum mousse

1²/3 cups dark chocolate,
    chopped
3 eggs
¹/4 cup superfine sugar

2 teaspoons dark rum
1 cup whipping cream, softly
    whipped

Stirring occasionally, heat the chocolate in a heatproof bowl over (not touching) a saucepan of simmering water until melted. Set aside to cool.

Using electric beaters, beat the eggs and sugar in a small bowl for 5 minutes or until thick, pale, and increased in volume.

Transfer the mixture to a large bowl. Using a metal spoon, fold in the melted chocolate with the rum. Leave the mixture to cool, then fold in the whipped cream until just combined.

Spoon into four 1-cup ramekins or dessert glasses. Refrigerate for 2 hours or until set.

Serves 4

zuppa inglese

4 thick slices sponge or pound
   cake
1/3 cup kirsch
1¼ cups raspberries
1¼ cups blackberries
2 tablespoons superfine sugar

1 cup vanilla custard
   (homemade or purchased)
1 cup whipping cream, lightly
   whipped
confectioners' sugar, to dust

Put a piece of sponge cake on each of four deep plates and brush or sprinkle it with the kirsch. Leave the kirsch to soak in for a minute or two.

Put the raspberries and blackberries in a saucepan with the superfine sugar. Gently warm through over low heat so that the sugar just melts, then leave the fruit to cool.

Spoon the fruit over the sponge cake, pour the custard on top of the berries, dollop the cream on top, and dust with confectioners' sugar. Serve immediately.

Serves 4

Panna cotta translates as "cooked cream"—a prosaic description for these silky smooth Italian baked custards.

vanilla bean liqueur panna cotta with liqueur berries

1¾ cups whipping cream
3 tablespoons superfine sugar
½ vanilla bean, split
2 teaspoons powdered gelatin
2 tablespoons Drambuie or
  similar liqueur (see notes)

2 cups mixed fresh or thawed
  frozen berries (see notes)
3 tablespoons confectioners'
  sugar
3 tablespoons Drambuie

Put the cream, sugar, and vanilla bean in a medium saucepan and stir to dissolve the sugar. Bring slowly just to a boil, then remove from the heat. Set aside for 5 minutes to cool a little.

Scrape the seeds from the vanilla bean into the mixture and discard the pod. Put the gelatin and 1 tablespoon cold water in a small bowl. Set over another bowl of hot water to dissolve the gelatin. Stir the dissolved gelatin into the creamy mixture and then stir in the liqueur. Strain the

mixture into a pitcher, then divide among four $^1/_2$-cup dariole, metal, or ceramic molds. Cover with plastic wrap, put on a tray, and refrigerate until set, at least 4 hours or overnight.

Meanwhile, combine the berries, confectioners' sugar, and Drambuie. Set aside for at least 1 hour so that the berries absorb the flavors and become juicy.

To remove the panna cottas from their molds, briefly dip the molds into hot water and loosen the edges with a small knife. Turn out onto serving plates. Serve with the berries and drizzle over some of the juice.

Notes: Drambuie is a Scotch whisky–based liqueur sweetened with honey and flavored with herbs. If using frozen berries, put them in a single layer on a shallow pan lined with paper towels and thaw in the refrigerator.

Serves 4

vanilla bean liqueur panna cotta
with liqueur berries

piña colada mousse

2 scant teaspoons powdered
    gelatin
1/4 cup piña colada (see note)
3 1/2 tablespoons butter
1/2 teaspoon pure vanilla extract
1 1/4 cups white chocolate, finely
    chopped
3 eggs, separated
1 egg white, extra

2 tablespoons superfine sugar
1/2 cup whipping cream,
    whipped
1/2 fresh coconut, to garnish
    (optional)
3 thin 1/8-inch slices peeled
    pineapple, to garnish
2 tablespoons fresh passion fruit
    pulp, to garnish

Mix the gelatin and half the piña colada in a small bowl. Put over a bowl of hot water and stir until dissolved. Melt the butter, vanilla, and remaining piña colada in a small saucepan over low heat. Remove from the heat and add the chocolate. Stir until the chocolate melts and the mixture is smooth. Stir in the gelatin. Transfer to a medium bowl and add the egg yolks one at a time, beating well after each addition. Cool.

Whisk the four egg whites until soft peaks form. Gradually add the sugar and continue whisking until firm peaks form. Using a metal spoon, fold a heaping spoonful of the whites into the chocolate mixture to loosen it, then gently fold in the remainder.

Carefully fold in the whipped cream. Spoon the mixture into 6 individual glass bowls, cover with plastic wrap, and refrigerate overnight.

If garnishing with the coconut, preheat the broiler to medium. Using a vegetable peeler, cut thin curling lengths from the outer edges of the coconut, including the brown skin. Spread on a cookie sheet and broil until crisp and lightly browned, 2–3 minutes (see notes).

Using a sharp knife, core and quarter the pineapple slices.

Top each glass of mousse with one or two coconut twists and a couple of pineapple pieces stuck in at a jaunty angle. Drizzle just a little passion fruit over the pineapple to serve.

Note: Instead of the piña colada, you can use 2 tablespoons each of pineapple juice and Malibu (coconut and rum liqueur). Unused coconut curls can be kept in an airtight container for many weeks then recrisped in the oven.

Serves 6

grand marnier soufflés with liqueur sabayon

superfine sugar, to sprinkle

1/4 cup butter, chopped
1/3 cup superfine sugar
1 tablespoon orange zest, grated
2 tablespoons all-purpose flour
1 tablespoon cornstarch
3 tablespoons Grand Marnier
    or other orange liqueur
1 cup milk
4 eggs, separated
2 egg whites, extra

liqueur sabayon
2 egg yolks
1/3 cup superfine sugar
1/3 cup Sauternes, white wine,
    or sweet sherry
1 tablespoon Grand Marnier or
    other orange liqueur

confectioners' sugar, to dust

Preheat the oven to 400°F. Grease six 1-cup soufflé dishes and sprinkle the sides and bottom with superfine sugar, tapping out the excess. Put the dishes on a cookie sheet.

Put the butter, sugar, and zest in a small bowl and beat with electric beaters for 2 minutes, until pale and creamy. Beat in the all-purpose flour, cornstarch, and liqueur.

Bring the milk to a boil in a medium saucepan. With beaters running, slowly pour the hot milk into the butter and flour mixture, beating constantly until smooth. Return the mixture to the saucepan and beat constantly over the heat until it boils and thickens. Beat in the egg yolks. Transfer to a large bowl.

Whisk the six egg whites in a large, clean bowl until soft peaks form. Use a metal spoon to stir one-third of the egg white into the other mixture, then carefully fold in the remaining white. Spoon into the prepared dishes. Bake for 15–18 minutes until well risen and cooked.

Meanwhile, make the liqueur sabayon. Put the egg yolks and sugar in a medium bowl and beat with electric beaters until creamy. Immerse the bowl in a large pan of simmering water and continue to beat for an additional 1 minute (take care that the cord of the beaters is kept well away from the flame). Pour in the wine or sherry and Grand Marnier. Beat for 5–7 minutes until tripled in volume and mousse-like. Remove from the heat and continue to beat for 1 minute. Pour into a serving pitcher.

Serve the soufflés immediately, dusted lightly with confectioners' sugar and with some sabayon poured into the center of each soufflé.

Serves 6

grand marnier soufflés with
liqueur sabayon

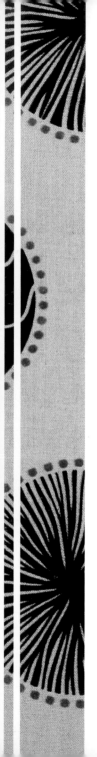

amaretti apple stack with caramel sauce

1 cup all-purpose flour	4 1/2 ounces almond cookies
2 eggs	(amaretti)
1 cup milk	5 cooking apples, peeled, cored,
2 tablespoons unsalted butter,	and very thinly sliced
melted	3/4 cup unsalted butter, melted
1 tablespoon Amaretto liqueur	1 cup light brown sugar,
(optional)	lightly packed
extra butter, for frying	1/2 cup dark corn syrup
	1/2 cup whipping cream
	3/4 cup light sour cream

Sift the flour into a large bowl and make a well in the center. Gradually whisk in the combined eggs and milk until the batter is smooth and free of lumps. Mix in the butter and Amaretto. Transfer to a pitcher, cover, and leave for 30 minutes to thicken.

Heat a small crêpe pan or nonstick frying pan and brush lightly with melted butter. Pour a little batter into the pan, swirl quickly to thinly cover the base, and pour any excess back into the pitcher. Cook for 30 seconds or until the edges just begin to curl, then turn and cook the other side until lightly browned. Transfer to a plate and cover with a clean cloth.

Repeat with the remaining batter to make 10 crêpes, greasing the pan when necessary. Stack the crêpes between parchment papers to prevent them from sticking together.

Preheat the oven to 350°F. Coarsely chop the amaretti in a food processor. Place on a cookie sheet. Stirring occasionally, bake until crisp, 5–8 minutes.

Mix the apple slices in a bowl with 1/4 cup of the melted butter and half the brown sugar. Spread evenly onto a shallow pan and place under a moderate broiler for 5 minutes. Turn and broil until light brown and soft (you may need to do this in batches). Set aside.

Put a crêpe on a large heatproof plate. Spread evenly with some apple, slightly mounded in the middle, and sprinkle with chopped amaretti. Continue to fill and layer in this manner until all the crêpes are stacked. Cover with foil and heat in the oven for 10 minutes or until warm.

Put the remaining brown sugar, syrup, cream, and remaining butter in a small pan. Stir over low heat until the sugar dissolves, then simmer for 1 minute. Spread the sour cream on the top crêpe. Pour a little warm sauce over the crêpe stack and cut into wedges to serve.

Serves 4–6

The sweet warmth of Cointreau gives bite to this simple upside-down dessert of pastry circles topped with orange slices.

orange galette with cointreau

2 prepackaged sheets puff
   pastry
3 1/2 tablespoons butter,
   softened
1/4 cup dark brown sugar,
   firmly packed

3 small oranges
2 teaspoons superfine sugar
2 teaspoons Cointreau or other
   orange liqueur

whipped cream, to serve

Cut a 9 1/2-inch circle from each of the pastry sheets. Put each on a cookie sheet, prick all over with a fork, and refrigerate until needed.

Grease two 9 1/2-inch metal pie pans (measured across the top). Cream the butter and dark brown sugar until the sugar dissolves. Divide the mixture between the prepared pans and spread it evenly over the bottoms. Chill while preparing the oranges.

Preheat the oven to 375°F. Using a vegetable peeler, remove and discard the zest from the oranges, leaving a good amount of pith on the orange.

Cut the oranges into thin, even slices, discarding any seeds. Don't use a serrated knife, as it will tear the flesh. Get rid of the juice by gently squeezing a stack of slices between your hands into the sink to remove as much juice as possible.

Arrange the slices, slightly overlapping, over the pastry bases. Sprinkle the superfine sugar and the Cointreau on top of each. Cover with the pastry circles, pricked side up. Bake on separate racks in the oven for 15 minutes, then flip them over and bake until the pastry is crisp and golden, 20–25 minutes. Don't worry if the pastry shrinks.

Remove the pastries from the oven, wait for 30–40 seconds, then quickly invert them onto flat plates. Put one on top of the other, with the oranges uppermost. Leave to settle for a minute, then serve immediately with whipped cream.

Serves 6–8

orange galette with cointreau

chestnut and rum swiss gâteau

cake
3 eggs
scant 1/2 cup superfine sugar
1/2 cup self-rising flour, sifted
1/2 teaspoon pure vanilla extract
31/2 tablespoons butter, melted
1–2 tablespoons superfine sugar,
   extra

filling
8 ounces (1 cup) unsweetened
   chestnut purée
1 egg yolk
2/3 cup confectioners' sugar
1–2 tablespoons strong rum
11/4 cups raspberries

frosting
1 small egg white
2 cups confectioners' sugar

Preheat the oven to 375°F. Lightly grease a 10 x 12-inch jelly roll pan and line the bottom with parchment paper.

For the cake, beat the eggs and sugar with electric beaters until thick, about 3 minutes. Fold in the flour, then the vanilla and butter. Pour into the prepared pan and bake until cooked through, about 12 minutes.

Sprinkle the extra sugar over a large sheet of parchment paper. As soon as the cake comes out of the oven, turn it out onto the sugared paper and peel off the parchment paper. Starting from one short end, roll the cake up into a log. Don't worry if a few cracks appear. Roll the paper around the log to secure the shape and leave to cool.

For the filling, blend the chestnut purée, egg yolk, and confectioners' sugar in a food processor until smooth. Beat in enough rum to give a soft and creamy consistency. The filling will taste very strongly of rum at this stage, but this will dissipate by the time the cake is served.

Unroll the cake, spread it with the filling, and sprinkle two-thirds of the raspberries over the top. Reroll. Put the roll on a serving plate with the cut edge underneath.

For the frosting, whisk the egg white lightly. Beat in the confectioners' sugar and enough warm water, half a teaspoon at a time, to make a soft frosting. Use this to lightly cover the roll with wavy peaks, then leave to set. To serve, cut into slices.

Serves 10

limoncello cream with tipsy ruby berries

3 small ladyfingers
2 tablespoons limoncello liqueur
   (see notes)

limoncello cream
2 eggs, separated
1/4 cup superfine sugar
2 tablespoons lemon zest,
   grated
3/4 cup whipping cream

berries
1 3/4 cups mixed fresh or frozen
   berries (see notes)
1/4 cup superfine sugar
2 tablespoons limoncello

2 tablespoons superfine sugar,
   extra
zest of 1 lemon (no pith), thinly
   shredded

Break the ladyfingers into small pieces and put them in a bowl. Sprinkle with the limoncello.

For the limoncello cream, beat the egg yolks and sugar until thick and creamy with electric beaters in another small bowl. Beat in the lemon zest. In another small bowl, use clean beaters to beat the egg whites until firm peaks form, then fold into the egg yolk mixture. Beat the cream until thick, then fold into the egg mixture. Cover and refrigerate at least 1 hour.

Meanwhile, put the mixed berries in a bowl. Sprinkle with the sugar and limoncello. Gently mix to combine. Set aside for 1 hour to allow the flavors to develop.

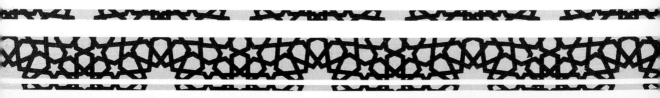

Put the extra sugar in a small saucepan with 3 tablespoons water. Stir to dissolve, then boil for 2 minutes to thicken a little. Add the shredded zest and cook for another 2 minutes. Remove the rind from the syrup and dry on paper towels. Set aside. Discard the syrup.

To assemble, place the soaked ladyfingers in the bottom of six decorative glass serving dishes of 1-cup capacity. Spoon the limoncello cream over, arrange the berries on top, and spoon some of the juice over. Sprinkle the shreds of lemon peel over the top of the cream and berries.

Notes: Limoncello is a lemon-flavored Italian liqueur. If using frozen berries, put them in a single layer on paper towels in a shallow pan and thaw in the refrigerator.

Serves 6

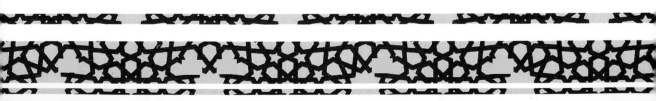

limoncello cream with tipsy ruby berries

chocolate kahlúa parfait

4^1/$_2$ ounces (1^1/$_4$ cups) chopped chocolate and vanilla cream cookies (about 11 cookies)
2 tablespoons Kahlúa or other coffee-flavored liqueur

1 cup whipping cream
2 cups chocolate ice cream
^{1}/$_3$ cup chocolate chips

Combine the cookies and the liqueur in a bowl. Set aside for 5 minutes for the cookies to absorb the liqueur.

Whip the cream until firm peaks form. In each of 4 tall parfait glasses, layer the ice cream, cookie mixture, cream, and chocolate chips, repeating until the glasses are full, ending with whipped cream and a few chocolate chips to garnish. Serve immediately.

Serves 4

almond cakes with red wine syrup

3/4 cup unsalted butter, chopped
1 cup superfine sugar
4 eggs
1 cup self-rising flour, sifted
1/3 cup ground almonds

1/3 cup milk
heavy cream, to serve

red wine syrup
1 1/2 cups superfine sugar
1 cup red wine
2/3 cup black currant juice

Preheat the oven to 400°F. Lightly grease six 1-cup capacity mini bundt pans and dust with flour, shaking out any excess.

Using electric beaters, cream the butter and sugar in a bowl until pale and fluffy. Add the eggs one at a time, beating well after each addition. Gently fold in the flour, then stir in the almonds and milk until just combined. Spoon into the prepared pans and bake for 15–20 minutes or until a skewer inserted into the center of a cake comes out clean. Remove from the oven and cool in the pan for 5 minutes, then turn out onto a wire rack.

For the syrup, put all the ingredients in a small saucepan and stir over low heat until the sugar dissolves. Increase the heat to medium and simmer for 10 minutes or until thick and syrupy. Serve the cakes with warm syrup poured over them and cream on the side.

Makes 6

This dessert is eaten firm, but will not freeze as hard as ice cream because it contains alcohol.

frozen chocolate whisky loaf

1¹/₃ cups good-quality dark
    chocolate, coarsely chopped
¹/₄ cup unsalted butter, softened
4 egg yolks
1¹/₄ cups whipping cream
2 teaspoons pure vanilla extract

2 tablespoons whisky
3 tablespoons unsweetened
    cocoa powder, to dust
whipped cream, to serve
wafer cookies, to serve

Line a 8¹/₂ x 5¹/₂-inch loaf pan with plastic wrap. In a heatproof bowl over a small saucepan of simmering water, simmer the chocolate, making sure that the base of the bowl does not touch the water. Stir the chocolate over the hot water until melted. Alternatively, melt the chocolate in a microwave oven for 1 minute on high, stirring after 30 seconds. Allow to cool.

Beat the butter and egg yolks in a small bowl until thick and creamy, then beat in the cooled chocolate mixture.

Using clean beaters, beat the cream and vanilla extract in a medium bowl until soft peaks form. Fold in the whisky. Using a metal spoon, fold the cream and chocolate mixtures together until just combined.

Pour the mixture into the prepared loaf pan, cover the surface with plastic wrap, and freeze for 2–3 hours, overnight, or until firm. Remove from the molds and carefully peel away the plastic wrap. Smooth the wrinkles on the surface of the loaf using a flat-bladed knife.

Place on a serving plate and dust with cocoa. If not serving immediately, return to the freezer for up to 1 week. Cut into slices to serve. The loaf can be served with extra cream and dessert wafers if desired.

Serves 6

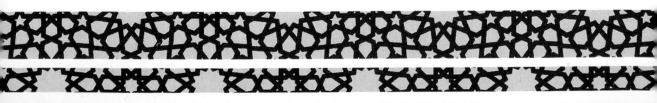

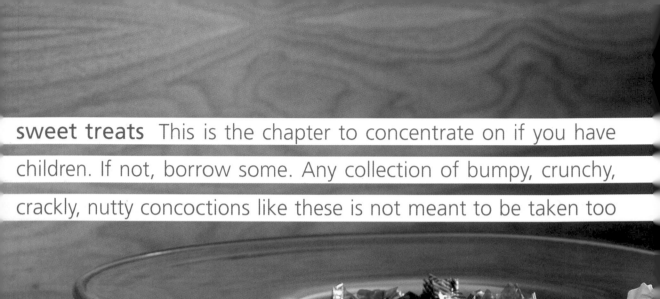

sweet treats This is the chapter to concentrate on if you have children. If not, borrow some. Any collection of bumpy, crunchy, crackly, nutty concoctions like these is not meant to be taken too

seriously. On the other hand . . . we all need to look after the child within every now and then, and rum truffles really are a mature taste. So free your inner child and go wild with sweet treats.

This chapter starts with a bang: honeycomb candy. If you didn't know it before, you soon will: honeycomb candy is really, terribly, wonderful for you. The first three ingredients are essentially sugar: superfine sugar, honey, and corn syrup. Then, 1 tablespoon of baking soda later and it's back to the sweet stuff, with a good helping of dark chocolate. And that's it. Well, so much for the first recipe, which fairly accurately sets the tone for what's to come. That is, an indulgent chapter of cookies, crisp wafers, and what can only be described as gooey, chocolatey, crunchy things. Sugar, in all its forms, appears with cheerful regularity, but also playing their part in this conspiracy to tempt us away from the straight and narrow are chocolate, cream, dried fruit, nuts, and alcohol. There is something for everyone here, from child-friendly food to sophisticated finishing touches for a dinner party. This chapter has classic accompaniments to tea and coffee, such as Florentines and creamy coconut ice. Quite a number of recipes that we probably shouldn't make, let alone eat, are also included, chief among them rocky road, but we should hasten to add that you're not meant to eat the whole thing in one sitting. White chocolate bark just begs to be investigated, whereas no-bake chocolate squares—well, obviously, you're making them for the kids. At heart, these are recipes for putting aside caution and just enjoying a mouthful or two of a little sweet something.

329

Add baking soda to sugar syrup and the foamy, brittle, sweet result is honeycomb candy—a little bit of kitchen alchemy.

honeycomb candy

1 1/2 cups superfine sugar	1 tablespoon baking soda
2 tablespoons honey	2/3 cup dark chocolate, chopped,
1/3 cup light corn syrup	to drizzle (optional)

Grease an 8 x 12-inch bar pan and line it with parchment paper, extending the paper over the long sides for easy removal later. Have a large metal bowl or saucepan ready, keeping in mind that the toffee will expand to triple its size when the baking soda is added.

Place the sugar, honey, syrup, and 1/4 cup water in a medium saucepan. Stir over low heat until the sugar dissolves, while using a pastry brush dipped in cold water to brush down the sides of the pan and remove any sugar crystals. Increase the heat to medium-high and boil the mixture without stirring until it reaches the hard crack stage on a candy thermometer (250°F) and turns light caramel in color, 7–8 minutes.

Now work quickly, as you need to retain the heat for the baking soda to aerate the toffee. Quickly pour the toffee into the large metal bowl, then immediately whisk in the baking soda. The mixture will very quickly rise and will continue to color with the heat. Pour it straight into the prepared pan. The mixture will continue to grow and expand at this stage. Roughly spread it out as best you can without disturbing the honeycomb too much, as this will disrupt the bubbling. Leave to cool until is it set, 20–30 minutes.

Cut the honeycomb candy into shards or rough squares. Heat the chocolate in a heatproof bowl over (not touching) a saucepan of gently simmering water, stirring frequently, until just melted and smooth. Brush one side of the honeycomb pieces with the chocolate, or spread them out and drizzle the chocolate over the pieces at random.

Store in an airtight container, as honeycomb candy will absorb any humidity from the air and become soggy.

Makes 4 cups

chocolate fruity nut clusters

²/₃ cup milk chocolate, chopped

²/₃ cup dark chocolate, chopped

¹/₂ cup toasted unsalted
macadamia nuts, halved

¹/₂ cup hazelnuts, toasted,
skinned, and halved (see
note, page 41)

¹/₃ cup candied ginger pieces,
chopped

¹/₃ cup dried apricots, chopped

¹/₃ cup sweetened dried
cranberries (see note)

Line 2 cookie sheets with foil. Put the chocolates in separate heatproof bowls and set them over (not touching) saucepans of simmering water. Stir until the chocolates are melted and smooth. Remove from the heat.

Combine the nuts and dried fruits. Stir half into each of the chocolates, mixing thoroughly. Set aside for 10 minutes to allow the chocolate to firm a little. Put small heaping spoonfuls onto the prepared trays. Refrigerate until firm. The clusters will keep in an airtight container for up to 2 weeks.

Note: Sweetened dried cranberries are sometimes sold as Craisins.

Makes 40

honey and nut chocolate wafers

7 tablespoons butter, cubed
3/4 cup superfine sugar
3 tablespoons honey
1/2 cup all-purpose flour
2 egg whites
1/2 cup unsalted macadamia
    nuts, halved

1/2 cup hazelnuts, toasted,
    skinned, and halved (see
    note, page 41)
1/2 cup dark chocolate, roughly
    chopped

Preheat the oven to 350°F. Lightly grease 3 large cookie sheets. (If you
have only one sheet, you will need to bake one batch at a time.) Cover
each with a sheet of parchment paper. In a food processor, process the
butter, sugar, honey, flour, and egg whites until well blended and smooth.

Using a metal spatula, spread one-third of the mixture thinly over the
entire surface of each cookie sheet. If the mixture is too difficult to spread,
tilt the sheet so that the mixture flows evenly over the base. Sprinkle each
batch with one-third of the combined macadamia nuts, hazelnuts, and
chocolate. Bake until evenly colored to a deep golden brown, 10–12
minutes. Cool on the tray until crisp, then break into large pieces. Store in
an airtight container and serve with coffee or on top of a creamy dessert.

Serves 12

honey and nut chocolate wafers

chocolate, nut, and ginger pâté

1²/₃ cups dark chocolate, chopped

1¹/₂ tablespoons butter

¹/₂ cup sweetened condensed milk

2 tablespoons rum or brandy

¹/₂ cup hazelnuts, toasted and skinned (see note, page 41)

¹/₂ cup unsalted macadamia nuts, toasted

¹/₃ cup whole almonds, toasted

¹/₃ cup candied ginger, finely chopped

Grease a 10 x 3¹/₄-inch loaf pan and line it with parchment paper. Extend the paper over the long sides for easy removal later.

Stirring frequently, heat the chocolate in a heatproof bowl over (not touching) a saucepan of gently simmering water until just melted and smooth. Add the butter, condensed milk, and rum or brandy. Stir until smooth. Remove from the heat, add the nuts and ginger, and mix thoroughly. Spoon into the prepared pan and smooth the surface. Cover and refrigerate several hours until firm. Cut into wafer-thin slices, and serve chilled with coffee. Store in the refrigerator; it will keep for 3 weeks.

Makes about 50 slices

peanut chews

scant 1/2 cup unsalted peanuts, toasted	2 tablespoons butter
heaping 1 cup sugar	2 tablespoons honey
1 cup whipping cream	2–3 drops pure vanilla extract

Line an 8-inch square pan with a double thickness of parchment paper. Extend the paper over two sides for easy removal later. Sprinkle the peanuts over the base. Put the sugar, cream, butter, honey, and vanilla into a heavy-bottomed saucepan and stir over low heat until the sugar dissolves. Using a pastry brush dipped in cold water, brush down the sides of the pan to remove any sugar crystals. Bring to a boil. Stirring occasionally, boil over medium-low heat until deep golden in color and a few drops form a semisoft ball when dropped into a bowl of cold water, 250°F on a candy thermometer. This will be the consistency of the finished chews, so cook the mixture for a little longer if it feels too soft.

Immediately pour the mixture over the peanuts in the prepared pan. Level the surface and leave to cool, about 2 hours. Lift out, using the paper as handles, and cut into logs using a buttered knife. Wrap the logs in cellophane, bonbon-style, to prevent them from sticking together.

Makes about 40

rum and raisin bagatelles

heaping 3/4 cup raisins
1 tablespoon Malibu (coconut
    and rum liqueur)
3/4 cup shredded coconut

2 2/3 cups dark chocolate,
    chopped
2/3 cup pine nuts, toasted

Put the raisins and Malibu in a small bowl, cover, and leave overnight.

Preheat the oven to 300°F. Spread the coconut on a paper-lined cookie sheet and bake until lightly golden, 5–10 minutes. Remove from the oven, lift the parchment paper and coconut off the sheet, and put to one side to cool. Line the cookie sheet with fresh parchment paper. Stirring frequently, heat the chocolate in a heatproof bowl over (not touching) a saucepan of gently simmering water until melted and smooth. Drain the raisins well. Remove the chocolate bowl from the heat and stir in the raisins, coconut, and pine nuts. Using greased teaspoons, take spoonfuls of mixture and shape into loose balls. Don't squash them too firmly—just enough for them to cling together, with bits of coconut and pine nuts sticking out. Put onto the prepared sheet. Leave to dry, then refrigerate until set completely. Store in an airtight container in the refrigerator for up to 2 weeks.

Makes about 32

white chocolate bark

1 cup unsalted macadamia nuts, toasted and chopped

2 cups white chocolate, chopped

2/3 cup dried apricots, finely chopped

1/3 cup dried currants

Preheat the oven to 350°F and line a cookie sheet with parchment paper. Spread the nuts over a second cookie sheet. Roast until lightly browned, 5–6 minutes, shaking the sheet once or twice to ensure even roasting. Allow to cool.

Heat the chocolate in a heatproof bowl over (not touching) a saucepan of simmering water until just melted and smooth. Remove from the heat. Add two-thirds of the nuts and dried fruit and stir to coat.

Pour the mixture into the prepared sheet and spread to a square of approximately 10 inches. Sprinkle over the remaining nuts and fruit. Cover with plastic wrap and refrigerate until set. Break into large chunks and store in an airtight container in the refrigerator. It will keep for 3 weeks.

Serves 8–10

white chocolate bark

no-bake chocolate squares

3 1/2 ounces shortbread cookies (about 7 cookies), roughly crushed

3/4 cup pistachios, shelled

1 cup hazelnuts, toasted and skinned (see note, page 41)

1/2 cup candied cherries, coarsely chopped

2 1/2 cups good-quality semisweet chocolate, chopped

scant 1 cup unsalted butter, chopped

1 teaspoon instant coffee granules

2 eggs, lightly beaten

Lightly grease a 7 x 10 1/2-inch baking pan and line with parchment paper, extending the paper over the two long sides for easy removal later. Combine the cookies, pistachios, about two-thirds of the hazelnuts, and half the cherries.

Stirring occasionally, heat the chocolate and butter in a heatproof bowl over (not touching) a saucepan of simmering water until melted and smooth. Remove from the heat. When the mixture has cooled slightly, mix in the coffee and eggs. Pour over the nut mixture and mix well. Pour the mixture into the pan and pat down well. Coarsely chop the remaining hazelnuts and sprinkle them over the top with the remaining cherries. Refrigerate overnight. Remove from the pan and trim the edges before cutting into pieces. Store in an airtight container in the refrigerator.

Makes 18

almond fruit bread

3 egg whites
heaping 1/2 cup superfine sugar
1 cup all-purpose flour, sifted
3/4 cup unblanched almond
   kernels

1/2 cup candied cherries
2 tablespoons candied apricots,
   cut into pieces the same size
   as the cherries
2 tablespoons candied
   pineapple, cut into pieces
   the same size as the almonds

Preheat the oven to 350°F. Grease a 10 x 3 1/4-inch loaf pan and line it with parchment paper. Whisk the egg whites in a medium bowl until soft peaks form, then gradually add the sugar, and continue whisking until very stiff peaks form. Fold through the flour. Gently fold in the almonds and dried fruits and pour into the prepared pan. Smooth the surface and bake until firm to touch, 30–40 minutes. Cool in the pan for 10 minutes, then turn out and peel off the parchment paper. Cool completely on a wire rack, then wrap in foil and set aside for 1–2 days.

Preheat the oven to 275°F and line a cookie sheet with parchment paper. Using a very sharp knife, cut the loaf into wafer-thin slices. Spread on the cookie sheet and bake until dry and crisp, 45–50 minutes. Cool on the sheet before storing in an airtight container.

Makes 30–40 slices

Praline—a mixture of nuts and toffee—gives a delicate crunch to these rich morsels.

praline liqueur-filled chocolate dates

praline filling
1/3 cup dark chocolate, chopped
2 tablespoons butter, softened
2 tablespoons Vienna almonds, chopped medium-fine (see notes)

1 tablespoon Grand Marnier or other orange liqueur
15 fresh dates (see notes)

1/3 cup milk chocolate, chopped

For the praline filling, put the chocolate in a heatproof bowl over (not touching) a saucepan of simmering water and stir until just melted and smooth. Remove from the heat and set aside to cool.

In a small bowl, whisk the butter until pale and creamy. Whisk in the melted chocolate, then add the chopped almonds and Grand Marnier. Cover and refrigerate until firm but not hard.

Use a small sharp knife to make a slit along each date and remove the pits. Put the praline filling in a small sturdy plastic bag and snip off a corner. Use as a pastry bag to fill the dates with the filling. Smooth off the filling along the cut edge with a small knife. Refrigerate on a tray.

Stirring frequently, heat the milk chocolate in a small heatproof bowl over (not touching) a saucepan of simmering water until just melted and smooth. Remove from the heat. Put the chocolate in a small, sturdy plastic bag and snip off a corner. Squiggle the chocolate across the dates in a decorative fashion.

Cover and refrigerate to firm the filling and to set the chocolate. Serve chilled. The dates will keep in the refrigerator in a covered container for 5 days.

Notes: Vienna almonds are almonds with a sugar coating; they are available in supermarkets or specialty nut or candy stores. You can use dried dates if fresh are not available.

Makes 15

praline liqueur-filled chocolate dates

fruit candies

1¹/3 cups dried apricots
1¹/3 cups dried pears, roughly
   chopped

2 cups sugar
heaping 1 cup sliced almonds,
   toasted

Put the apricots and pears in separate saucepans and generously cover with water. Bring to a boil over low to medium heat and simmer until tender, about 40 minutes. Check the water levels from time to time and add hot water if necessary to prevent the fruit from sticking to the pans.

When the fruit is tender, increase the heat and quickly boil off any excess water in the pans (otherwise the texture of the candies will be more jam-like rather than firm). Remove from the heat, add 1 cup sugar to each pan, and stir until the sugar melts. Put on a low heat and bring to a boil. Stirring often, simmer for 25–30 minutes, until the mixture comes away from the sides of the pan, but its texture is still a little chunky.

Line two 2³/4 x 8¹/4-inch loaf pans with parchment paper. Pour the apricots into one pan, the pears into the other. Leave overnight to firm up.

Put the almonds into a shallow bowl and break them up a little with your hands. Using a knife dipped in cold water, cut the fruit slabs into short fingers and toss them in the almonds. The candies will keep in an airtight container for many weeks.

Makes about 60

rum truffles

1 1/3 cups dark chocolate, finely chopped
1/4 cup whipping cream
2 tablespoons butter
1/3 cup chocolate cake, crumbled

2 teaspoons dark rum, brandy or whisky
1/2 cup chocolate sprinkles

Line a cookie sheet with foil. Put the chocolate in a heatproof bowl. Combine the cream and butter in a small saucepan and stir over low heat until the butter melts and the mixture is just boiling. Pour the mixture over the chocolate and stir until the chocolate is melted and smooth.

Stir in the cake crumbs and rum. Stirring occasionally, refrigerate for 20 minutes or until firm enough to handle. Roll heaping teaspoons of the mixture into balls.

Spread the chocolate sprinkles on a sheet of parchment paper. Roll each truffle in the sprinkles until evenly coated, then place on the cookie sheet. Alternatively, the truffles can be rolled in unsweetened cocoa powder. Refrigerate for 30 minutes or until firm.

Makes about 25

The Turkish name of this confection translates evocatively as "rest for the throat"—what could be more enticing?

turkish delight

1/4 cup powdered gelatin	pink food coloring
2 cups sugar	heaping 3/4 cup confectioners'
1/2 teaspoon lemon juice	sugar, sifted and combined
1 strip lemon zest, no pith	with 3 tablespoons
1/2 teaspoon tartaric acid	cornstarch, to coat
1–1 1/2 teaspoons rose water,	
or to taste	

Put 2 1/2 cups cold water in a heavy-bottom saucepan and sprinkle in the gelatin. Put over low heat and stir until the gelatin dissolves. Add the sugar, lemon juice, and lemon zest and continue stirring until the sugar dissolves. Bring to a boil and boil for 8 minutes, stirring constantly. Discard the lemon zest.

Brush a 7 x 4-inch loaf pan with water.

Stir the tartaric acid and rose water into the mixture. Add the food coloring, 2–3 drops at a time, until a very pale pink is reached. Pour into the prepared pan and leave overnight to set (do not refrigerate).

Dust 3–4 tablespoons of the confectioners' sugar mixture on a cold hard surface (marble is ideal) and put the rest into a shallow bowl. Ease the Turkish delight away from the sides of the pan with your fingers. Starting at one end, peel it out of the pan. It tends to be sticky and will stretch a little, but it is quite resilient. Place the slab on the sugar-covered work surface.

Using a greased knife, cut the Turkish delight into 1-inch squares and toss them in the bowl of confectioners' sugar mixture to coat all sides. Work with a few at a time to prevent the uncoated pieces from sticking together. Store in an airtight container, with parchment paper between each layer. It will keep for many weeks.

Makes 36

351

turkish delight

florentines

1/4 cup butter, cubed
1/2 cup superfine sugar
1/2 cup whipping cream
1 cup slivered almonds
1/3 cup candied cherries, finely
    chopped
1/3 cup mixed candied peel

1/4 cup candied ginger, finely
    chopped
1/3 cup all-purpose flour

2/3 cup dark chocolate, chopped
2/3 cup white chocolate,
    chopped

Preheat the oven to 315°F. Line a large cookie sheet with parchment paper. Put the butter, sugar, and cream in a small saucepan and stir over low heat until smooth and combined. Bring just to a boil, then remove from the heat.

Combine the almonds, cherries, mixed peel, ginger, and flour in a medium bowl. Stir in the butter mixture. Set aside for 5 minutes for the mixture to thicken a little.

Put small heaping teaspoonfuls, well spaced, onto the prepared sheet. Flatten each to a 2-inch round. You will need to bake the cookies in several batches. Bake until a dark golden brown, 12–15 minutes. Cool each batch on the sheet, then transfer to a wire rack to cool completely and become crisp.

Put the dark and white chocolates in separate heatproof bowls and set each bowl over (not touching) a saucepan of simmering water. Stir until the chocolates are just melted and smooth. Remove from the heat.

Using a metal spatula, coat the underside of half the cookies with the dark chocolate and the remaining half with the white chocolate. Mark the chocolate with wavy lines using a fork, if desired. Put the cookies on a wire rack, chocolate side up, to set.

Store in an airtight container for up to 5 days.

355

Makes 45

rocky road

2³/4 cups pink and white
  marshmallows, halved
1 cup unsalted peanuts, coarsely
  chopped

¹/2 cup candied cherries, halved
1 cup shredded coconut
2¹/3 cups dark chocolate,
  chopped

Line the base and two opposite sides of a shallow 8-inch square cake pan with foil.

Put the marshmallows, peanuts, cherries, and coconut into a large bowl and mix until well combined.

Stirring occasionally, heat the chocolate in a heatproof bowl over (not touching) a bowl of simmering water until just melted and smooth. Add the chocolate to the marshmallow mixture and toss until well combined. Spoon into the cake pan and press evenly over the bottom. Refrigerate for several hours or until set. Carefully lift it out of the pan, then peel away the foil and cut the rocky road into 2-inch squares. Store in an airtight container in the refrigerator.

Serves 16

creamy coconut ice

2 cups confectioners' sugar
1/4 teaspoon cream of tartar
14-ounce can sweetened
   condensed milk

31/2 cups dried grated coconut
2–3 drops pink food coloring

Grease an 8-inch square cake pan and line the bottom and 2 opposite sides with parchment paper, extending the paper over the sides for easy removal later.

Sift the confectioners' sugar and cream of tartar into a bowl. Make a well in the center and add the condensed milk. Using a wooden spoon, stir in half the coconut, then the remaining coconut. Mix well, using your hands. Divide the mixture in half and tint one half pink. Using your hands, knead the color through evenly.

Press the pink mixture evenly over the bottom of the pan, then cover with the white mixture and press down firmly. Refrigerate for 1–2 hours or until firm. Remove from the pan, remove the paper, and cut into 2 x 1-inch rectangles. Store in an airtight container in a cool place for up to 3 weeks

Serves 32

creamy coconut ice

These chocolate-coated confections are sure to be popular,

so it's just as well the recipe makes a generous quantity.

chewy caramel and walnut logs

1/2 cup butter, cubed
14-ounce can sweetened
   condensed milk
2 tablespoons cane syrup or
   unsulfured molasses

1 3/4 cup light brown sugar,
   firmly packed
3/4 cup walnuts, toasted and
   finely chopped
1 3/4 cups dark chocolate,
   chopped

Grease a 7-inch square cake pan and line it with parchment paper, extending it over 2 opposite sides for easy removal later.

Stir the butter, condensed milk, cane syrup, and brown sugar in a medium saucepan over low heat until the butter melts and the sugar dissolves. Increase the heat a little so that the mixture bubbles at a steady slow boil. Stir constantly until caramel in color and the mixture leaves the sides of the pan when stirred, 9–10 minutes. Stir in the walnuts. Pour into the prepared pan and leave at room temperature to cool and set.

Remove from the pan using the parchment paper for handles. Cut into 6 even pieces. Gently roll each piece into a log approximately 4^1/$_2$ inches long and place on a tray lined with parchment paper. Refrigerate until firm, about 1 hour.

Melt the chocolate in a small bowl over a saucepan of simmering water, ensuring that the water doesn't touch the bottom of the bowl. Coat each caramel log with the chocolate and put back onto the tray. Return to the refrigerator until set.

About 10 minutes before serving, take as many logs as are needed at the time from the refrigerator. Cut into slices about ^{1}/$_2$ inch thick.

Store in an airtight container in the refrigerator for up to 1 week.

Makes about 70 pieces

sugared fruit cups

a selection of 20 pieces of small fruit of a uniform size, with stalks attached (such as large green and purple grapes, cherries, gooseberries)

3/4 cup pure confectioners' sugar, sifted
1 tablespoon Pear William, or other fruit-based liqueur
about 1 teaspoon lemon juice
2–3 teaspoons superfine sugar

Snip grapes from the bunch, each with its stalk attached. Pull the dried leaves of gooseberries up and twist them together to form a fat stalk.

In a small bowl, stir together the confectioners' sugar and liqueur. Add the lemon juice, a few drops at a time, until a thick, slowly flowing frosting forms. Spread the superfine sugar in a saucer. Working with 5–6 pieces of fruit at a time, hold each piece by the stalk and dip it in the frosting to cover the bottom three-quarters. Gently shake off the excess. Set it on a plate to dry a little. When you have 5–6 pieces, roll each in the sugar, starting with the first piece that you dipped. If the frosting forms waves and doesn't allow an even coating of sugar, leave the fruit for little longer to dry more before sugaring. Set the pieces on a clean plate while you coat the remainder. When the frosting is dry, set the fruits in small foils or paper chocolate cases. They will keep covered in the refrigerator for up to 4 days.

Makes 20

dark chocolate nutty fudge

2 cups superfine sugar
2/3 cup evaporated milk
2 tablespoons butter
1 cup white marshmallows
12/3 cups dark chocolate,
   chopped

1 cup unsalted mixed nuts,
   toasted and coarsely
   chopped
1/2 cup white chocolate,
   chopped

Grease a 7-inch square cake pan and line it with parchment paper. Heat the sugar, milk, and butter in a medium saucepan over low heat until the sugar dissolves. Increase the heat to medium and bring to a boil. Stirring, simmer for 4–5 minutes. Remove from the heat and stir in the marshmallows and dark chocolate. Continue stirring until smooth, adding the nuts at the end. Pour into the prepared pan and refrigerate until set.

Melt the white chocolate in a small bowl over (not touching) a saucepan of simmering water. Remove the chocolate nut mixture from the pan and cut into 16 squares. Put the squares on a sheet of parchment paper and, using a pastry bag, pipe the white chocolate in drizzly lines over the squares. Allow the white chocolate to set before storing or eating. Store in an airtight container in the refrigerator. Before eating, bring out and leave at room temperature for 10 minutes to allow it to soften slightly.

Makes 16 pieces

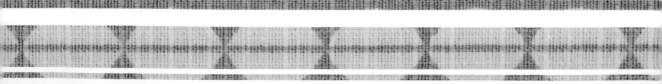

dark chocolate nuttty fudge

sugar and spice Look not for a plain cake with a token swipe of frosting in this chapter. Oh, no—sweet creamy fillings, luscious toppings, and syrupy sauces are here to demonstrate the many delicious lengths to which versatile sugar can be taken. Spices provide a fragrant and exotic contrasting note, while butterscotch, coffee, caramel, nuts, and other decadent flavors round it all out.

Experimentation is the order of the day here. If previous chapters have concentrated on the many ways in which the "front of the cupboard" ingredients—such as flour, sugar, cocoa, and eggs—can be combined to produce delicious desserts, this chapter positively encourages a little rummaging around in back. Where else is the green ginger wine or the can of sweetened condensed milk to be found? These are not ingredients used every day, but that doesn't mean to say that when they are used, they don't shine. Made from a blend of grapes and pure root ginger, green ginger wine adds a distinct sweet-sharp note to a creamy ginger and nut log. Fresh lavender flowers transform an otherwise classic pancake batter into something altogether more fragrant and exotic. The other side of this chapter is sugar, in the form of sauces, creams, and syrups. They include butterscotch and caramel sauce, toffee (plain and brandied), white chocolate cream frosting, citrus syrup for soaking into cakes, vanilla cream dolloped on the side, and thick coffee cream sandwiched between nutty meringue layers. Sweet desserts made sweeter still. The task of bringing all these elements together in perfect harmony falls to nuts, those great double-agents of the kitchen, able to do savory and sweet with equal aplomb. So, when everyday staples just don't provide the magic you are after, a little sugar and spice will.

butterscotch meringue pie

piecrust pastry
2 cups all-purpose flour
1/2 cup unsalted butter, chilled
   and chopped
2 tablespoons superfine sugar
1 egg yolk
1 tablespoon ice water

butterscotch filling
1 cup soft brown sugar, lightly
   packed
1/3 cup all-purpose flour

1 cup milk
3 tablespoons unsalted butter
1 teaspoon pure vanilla extract
1 egg yolk

meringue
2 egg whites
2 tablespoons superfine sugar

Preheat the oven to 350°F. Grease a deep 8 1/2-inch pie pan. Sift the flour into a large bowl and rub in the butter with your fingertips until the mixture resembles bread crumbs. Stir in the sugar, yolk, and water. Mix to a soft dough, then gather into a ball. Wrap in plastic wrap and chill for 20 minutes.

Roll the pastry between two sheets of parchment paper until it is large enough to cover the bottom and sides of the pan. Transfer to the pan, pressing it in gently. Trim the edge and prick the pastry evenly with a fork. Chill again for 20 minutes. Line the pastry with a sheet of parchment paper and spread pastry weights or uncooked beans or rice over the paper. Bake for 35 minutes, then remove the paper and weights.

For the filling, place the sugar and flour in a small pan. Make a well in the center and gradually whisk in the milk to form a smooth paste. Add the butter and whisk over low heat for 8 minutes or until the mixture boils and thickens. Remove from the heat, add the vanilla and egg yolk, and whisk until smooth. Spread into the pastry case and smooth the surface.

For the meringue, beat the egg whites until stiff peaks form. Add the sugar gradually, beating until thick and glossy and all the sugar has dissolved. Spoon over the filling and swirl it into peaks with a fork or flat-bladed knife. Bake for 5–10 minutes or until the meringue is golden. Serve warm or cold.

Serves 8–10

France's Normandy region is famed for its apples and cream, so any dish labeled "Normande" will feature these ingredients.

crêpes normandes

crème Normande
3/4 cups whipping cream
1 teaspoon confectioners' sugar, sifted
1–2 teaspoons Calvados (apple brandy)

crêpes
1/2 cup all-purpose flour
1 egg
3/4 cup milk
1/2 teaspoon pure vanilla extract
1 large Granny Smith apple
1/2 cup unsalted butter
2/3 cup superfine sugar

Combine the cream, confectioners' sugar, and Calvados in a small bowl. Set aside while you make the crêpes (the cream will thicken a little).

For the crêpes, sift the flour and a small pinch of salt into a bowl. Combine the egg, milk, and vanilla in a small bowl. Pour the liquid into the flour and whisk lightly until just combined.

Peel, core, quarter, and very thinly slice the apple (use a mandoline if you have one). Melt a little butter in a crêpe pan over low to medium heat and add 5–6 apple slices. Fry without turning until they begin to darken, about 2 minutes.

Ladle a thin coating of batter over the top of the apples and cook for 50–60 seconds. Sprinkle with a tablespoon of sugar and cook until the sugar melts, 50–60 seconds. Add more butter; when it has melted, flip the crêpe over. Continue cooking until the crêpe is crisp, about 45 seconds. Slide onto a plate and keep warm while cooking 5 more crêpes in the same way, wiping the pan clean with a paper towel after each crêpe.

Serve warm, drizzled with the cream mixture.

Serves 6

crêpes normandes

Ground hazelnuts give this meringue roll an interesting texture, and also serve to make it less sweet than the usual meringue.

hazelnut crackle log

1/2 cup hazelnuts toasted and
    skinned (see note, page 41)
4 egg whites, at room
    temperature
2/3 cup superfine sugar
1 teaspoon cornstarch
1 teaspoon pure vanilla extract
1 teaspoon white wine vinegar

filling
2 teaspoons instant coffee
    granules
2 teaspoons hot water
1 cup mascarpone cheese
2 tablespoons confectioners'
    sugar

For the meringue, preheat the oven to 300°F. Draw an 8 x 14-inch rectangle on a sheet of parchment paper. Put the sheet, pencil side down, on a cookie sheet.

Put the hazelnuts in a food processor and process until coarsely ground.

Whisk the egg whites in a large bowl until soft peaks form. Gradually add the sugar, 1 tablespoon at a time, and whisk until stiff and glossy. Gently fold in the hazelnuts, then the cornstarch, vanilla, and vinegar. Spoon onto the cookie sheet and spread evenly inside the marked rectangle. Bake for 25 minutes or until the meringue is set and lightly golden.

Lay a large sheet of parchment paper on a work surface and invert the cooked meringue on top. Peel off the parchment paper that was used to line the cookie sheet and set the meringue aside to cool for 15 minutes.

To make the filling, dissolve the instant coffee in the hot water. Put the coffee, mascarpone, and confectioners' sugar in a bowl and mix well.

Using a spatula, spread the filling evenly over the meringue. Starting at one short end and using the parchment paper as a lever, gently roll up the meringue. The outer surface will crack into a pattern. Serve immediately, cut into slices.

Serves 8–10

chilled strawberry liqueur soufflé with strawberry compote

soufflé
1²/3 cups strawberries, hulled

3 tablespoons strawberry or
   raspberry liqueur

4 teaspoons powdered
   gelatin

4 eggs, separated

²/3 cup superfine sugar

1 cup whipping cream

3 tablespoons superfine sugar,
   extra

strawberry compote
2 tablespoons confectioners'
   sugar

2 tablespoons strawberry or
   raspberry liqueur

1²/3 cups strawberries, hulled
   and chopped

Grease a 5-cup soufflé dish and sprinkle with superfine sugar. Tap out the excess. Put a collar on the dish (see note). Set the dish on a flat sheet.

Purée the strawberries and liqueur in a food processor. Set aside. Put the gelatin in a small bowl with 2 tablespoons cold water. Set the bowl over another bowl of hot water to dissolve the gelatin.

In a medium bowl, whisk together the egg yolks and superfine sugar. Put the bowl over a saucepan of simmering water and whisk until thick and pale, 2–3 minutes. Stir in the gelatin mixture and set aside to just cool, stirring occasionally.

Fold the strawberry purée into the gelatin mixture. Beat the cream until firm, then fold into the gelatin and strawberry mixture.

In a clean bowl, whisk the egg whites until soft peaks form. Whisking constantly, gradually add the 3 tablespoons extra superfine sugar. Beat until firm but not stiff, 1–2 minutes. Gently fold the egg white into the strawberry and cream mixture. Spoon into the prepared dish and smooth the surface. (The mixture will be above the rim of the dish.) Refrigerate until firm, at least 3 hours.

For the compote, stir the sugar and liqueur in a medium saucepan over low heat until dissolved, then add the strawberries and toss through until warmed. To serve, carefully remove the paper collar from the soufflé. Spoon onto serving plates and serve with the compote.

Note: For the collar, cut a sheet of parchment paper long enough to wrap around the dish. Fold it lengthwise into thirds. Lightly grease the inside of the dish. Position the collar so that it protrudes 3 inches above the dish and tie in position with jute or cotton (not plastic) string.

Serves 6–8

chilled strawberry liqueur soufflé with
strawberry compote

mini pastries with chocolate and vanilla cream

choux pastry
3 tablespoons butter, cubed
1/2 cup all-purpose flour
2 eggs, lightly beaten
2 tablespoons sliced almonds

chocolate cream
1/2 cup milk
1/4 cup dark chocolate, chopped
1 egg yolk
1 tablespoon superfine sugar

vanilla cream
1/2 cup milk
1/2 vanilla bean, split
1 egg yolk
1 tablespoon superfine sugar

3/4 cup whipping cream
1 tablespoon confectioners' sugar
confectioners' sugar, to dust

Preheat the oven to 425°F. On a large sheet of parchment paper, mark out four 3 1/2-inch rounds. Lightly grease a cookie sheet and line with the parchment paper, pencil side down.

For the pastry, put the butter and 1/2 cup water in a medium saucepan and gently heat until the butter melts. Bring to a boil over medium heat, then remove from the heat and add the flour, mixing well with a wooden spoon to combine. Return to the heat. Stirring, cook until the mixture leaves the sides of the pan and forms a ball.

Transfer the mixture to a medium bowl and gradually beat in the eggs using electric beaters. Continue beating until smooth and glossy. Transfer to a large pastry bag with a plain piping tip. Pipe circular mounds of mixture inside the lines drawn on the paper. Sprinkle the tops with almonds. Bake for 10 minutes, reduce the temperature to 350°F, and bake until puffed and golden, about 15 minutes. Cut in half using a serrated knife and bake until the centers are dry, 3–5 minutes more. Cool on a wire rack while you make the creams.

For the chocolate cream, heat the milk and chocolate in a small saucepan over low heat, stirring, until the chocolate melts. Bring almost to boiling point, then remove from the heat. Mix the egg yolk and sugar in a small bowl, then gradually add the hot milk, whisking continually. Pour the mixture back into the saucepan and stir over low heat until thickened. Pour into a serving pitcher and cool.

For the vanilla cream, put the milk in a small saucepan. Scrape the seeds from the vanilla bean into the milk, then add the bean also. Bring almost to boiling point, then remove from the heat. Mix the egg yolk and sugar in a small bowl, then gradually add the hot milk, whisking continually. Pour the mixture back into the saucepan and stir over low heat until thickened. Strain into a serving pitcher and cool.

When ready to serve, whip the cream until firm peaks form, gradually adding the confectioners' sugar toward the end. Use this mixture to fill the pastries. Set a pastry on each of four serving plates, dust with confectioners' sugar, and serve at once. Serve with the pitchers of creams on the side.

Makes 4

hazelnut and coffee meringue torte

meringue
2²/3 cups hazelnuts, toasted and
   skinned (see note, page 41)
8 egg whites
heaping ³/4 cup superfine sugar
¹/3 cup all-purpose flour
1 cup dark chocolate, chopped

filling
¹/4 cup confectioners' sugar
1¹/2 tablespoons instant coffee
   granules
2 cups whipping cream

Preheat the oven to 300°F. Draw an 8¹/2-inch circle on each of 3 sheets of parchment paper. Lay one sheet, pencil side down, on each of 3 cookie sheets.

In a food processor, pulse the hazelnuts until chopped to a medium-coarse texture. Reserve ¹/4 cup for later.

In a large bowl, whisk the egg whites until stiff peaks form. Gradually add the sugar, whisking constantly until thick and glossy. Gently fold in the flour and nuts.

Divide the mixture among the sheets, spreading it out evenly to the drawn circles. Bake until light golden brown, 25–30 minutes. They will be cakelike, not like a typical crisp meringue. If you use 3 oven racks, the sheets will need to be swapped around during cooking for even browning. Cool on the sheets, then gently peel off the parchment paper.

Meanwhile, melt the chocolate in a small bowl over a saucepan of simmering water, ensuring that the water doesn't touch the bottom of the bowl. Spread one-third of the chocolate over each of 2 meringue circles. Refrigerate the meringue circles while the filling is being made.

In a medium bowl, dissolve the confectioners' sugar and coffee in 1^1/$_2$ tablespoons warm water. Add the cream and whip until thick.

Put one chocolate-coated meringue layer onto a serving plate, chocolate side up. Spread with one-third of the filling, leaving the edges uncovered—the filling will ooze out as the layers are added. Repeat the layering. Put the plain meringue on top and spread with the last one-third of filling. Sprinkle with the reserved hazelnuts. Spoon the remaining melted chocolate into a small pastry bag (or a sturdy plastic bag with one corner snipped off) and drizzle decorative stripes across the cream and nuts.

Serves 8

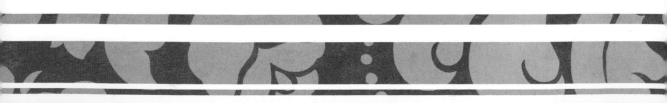

hazelnut and coffee meringue torte

almond, orange, and quince tarts

pastry
1 1/4 cups all-purpose flour

heaping 1/3 cup confectioners' sugar

7 tablespoons unsalted butter, cubed

1 egg yolk

3–4 drops pure vanilla extract

filling
1/2 cup superfine sugar

1/3 cup unsalted butter, softened

2 eggs

2 teaspoons orange zest, finely grated

1/2 cup ground almonds

1 cup slivered almonds, toasted

3 1/2 ounces (1 cup) quince paste, thinly sliced

For the pastry, process the flour, confectioners' sugar, butter, egg yolk, and vanilla in a food processor until just smooth. Form into a ball, cover with plastic wrap, and chill for 45 minutes.

Grease six 3 1/4-inch loose-bottom tart pans. Roll the pastry out thinly on a lightly floured surface and use it to line the prepared pans. Chill the pastry-lined pans while the oven preheats.

Preheat the oven to 350°F. Line the pastry pans with parchment paper, cover the bottom of each with pastry weights or dried beans or rice, and bake for 10 minutes. Remove the parchment paper and weights and return to the oven for 5 minutes. Cool while making the filling.

For the filling, beat the sugar and butter together until smooth, then add the eggs one at a time, beating well after each addition. Don't worry if the mixture separates. Stir through the orange zest and the ground and slivered almonds.

Place the quince paste slices in the bottom of each tart shell, dividing them evenly among the tart shells. Divide the filling among the pastry cases and bake until set, about 20 minutes.

Serve warm with whipped cream or vanilla bean ice cream.

Makes 6

caramel tarts with chocolate ganache

ganache
²/₃ cup dark chocolate, chopped
2 tablespoons whipping cream

pastry
1¹/₄ cups all-purpose flour
¹/₃ cup unsalted butter, chilled
   and cubed
heaping ¹/₄ cup superfine sugar

filling
14-ounce can sweetened
   condensed milk
2 tablespoons unsalted butter
2 tablespoons cane syrup or
   unsulfured molasses
1¹/₂ tablespoons shelled
   pistachios, to garnish (see
   note)

For the ganache, melt the chocolate and cream in a bowl over a saucepan of simmering water, stirring well to combine. Remove from the heat, cool, then refrigerate until firm but not solid, 10–15 minutes.

Preheat the oven to 350°F. Grease a 12-hole cupcake pan (each hole 3 tablespoons capacity). Run a strip of foil across the bottom and up two sides of each hole, leaving a bit of overhang. These will act as handles to aid removal of the tarts later on.

For the pastry, put the flour, butter, and sugar into a food processor and process until the mixture resembles bread crumbs. Divide among the prepared cupcake pan holes; firmly press the mixture down onto the

bottom with your fingers. Bake until lightly golden, 12–15 minutes. While they are still hot, press the bottoms down with the back of a small teaspoon, as they will have risen a little.

For the filling, put the condensed milk, butter, and syrup in a small saucepan over low heat. Stir until the butter melts. Increase the heat to medium and simmer, stirring constantly, until light caramel in color, 2–3 minutes. When stirring, ensure that the bottom and sides of the pan are scraped to prevent the mixture from catching and scorching.

Divide the caramel among the pastry cases and cool for 5 minutes. Gently remove the tarts from the pan; transfer to a wire rack to cool completely.

To serve, whisk the ganache well. Put into a pastry bag with a medium-sized star tip and pipe swirls of ganache on top of the caramel. Sprinkle with the pistachios. Store in the refrigerator covered; remove from the refrigerator 10–15 minutes before eating.

Note: The pistachios can be toasted in the oven after the tart crusts bake.

Makes 12

caramel tarts with
chocolate ganache

creamy ginger and nut log

filling
scant 1/2 cup superfine sugar
7 tablespoons butter, softened
2 cups farmer cheese or
    Neufchâtel
1/2 teaspoon orange zest, grated
1/2 teaspoon lemon zest, grated
1 teaspoon pure vanilla extract
1 egg
1/4 cup pecans
1 ounce (1 1/2 tablespoons)
    candied ginger

cookie layers
about 24 small 3 1/4-inch long
    ladyfingers
about 1/2 cup green ginger wine

chocolate glaze
1 cup dark chocolate
2 tablespoons green ginger
    wine
1/4 cup superfine sugar
3 tablespoons butter, cubed

For the filling, process the sugar and butter in a food processor until pale. Add the cheese and process until smooth. Transfer to a bowl, add the zests, vanilla, and egg and mix well. Chop the pecans and ginger to a medium-fine texture and fold through the cheese mixture.

To assemble, run a double thickness of foil across the bottom of a 3 1/4 x 6 1/4-inch loaf pan, allowing for plenty of overhang to remove the loaf later on. Line the bottom with a single layer of ladyfingers, flat side down (the length of the cookies should run the length of the pan). If necessary, trim the cookies to fit snugly. Sprinkle liberally with green ginger wine, but not so much that the cookies become soggy. Line both sides of the pan with a single layer of cookies in a similar manner, flat side out and running in the same direction as those on the bottom. Sprinkle with more green ginger wine. Spread one-half of the filling over them, packing it in firmly, and cover this with another layer of cookies. Sprinkle with more green ginger wine. Spread the remaining filling on top and cover with the last of the cookies, this time with the flat side uppermost. The filling and cookies should end up on the same level; trim the cookies if necessary. Sprinkle with the last of the wine. Wrap the pan in foil and leave in the refrigerator overnight to set.

For the chocolate glaze, melt the chocolate with the ginger wine in a bowl over a pan of simmering water, stirring occasionally until smooth. Remove from the heat and stir in the superfine sugar, then the butter; stir until smooth and glossy. If necessary, beat in a little water, a teaspoon at a time, to give a spoonable consistency.

Turn the loaf out onto a wire cake rack set over a tray. Remove the foil, then spoon the glaze all over, completely covering the top and sides. Leave until set (the glaze will remain slightly soft). Cut into slices to serve.

Serves 8

blueberry and lavender pancake stack

raspberry coulis
2/3 cup fresh raspberries
1 tablespoon honey
1 teaspoon lemon juice

maple cream
1 1/2 cups crème fraîche
2–3 tablespoons pure maple
syrup

pancakes
1 teaspoon lemon zest, grated
2 tablespoons whipping cream

1 egg, separated
2/3 cup milk
1/3 cup all-purpose flour
2 teaspoons superfine sugar
1 teaspoon organic lavender
flowers (stripped off the
stalk)
1 cup fresh blueberries

unsalted butter, for frying
a few organic lavender flowers,
extra to garnish

For the raspberry coulis, process the raspberries, honey, and lemon juice in a food processor until smooth. Pass through a fine sieve; discard the seeds.

For the maple cream, beat the crème fraîche and maple syrup together until smooth.

For the pancakes, mix together the lemon zest, cream, egg yolk, and milk in a small bowl. Sift the flour into a bowl. Stir in the sugar and lavender flowers and pour in the liquid. Whisk to a smooth batter.

In a clean bowl, whisk the egg white until stiff. Using a metal spoon, gently fold the egg white into the batter.

Melt a small pat of butter in a crêpe pan or nonstick frying pan. Spoon in enough batter, roughly 1^1/$_2$ tablespoons, to make a 3^1/$_4$-inch pancake and sprinkle some blueberries on top. When small bubbles begin to break on the surface, flip the pancake over. Fry for another minute or two, until golden on both sides and cooked through. Transfer to a warm plate and keep covered. Once you get used to it you can make 3 or 4 pancakes at once. Repeat, using up all the batter, and wiping the pan clean with a paper towel between each batch of pancakes. You will need 12 pancakes; there is enough batter to allow for a couple of failures.

Put a pancake on each of 4 serving plates and top with a heaping tablespoon of maple cream. Repeat twice more, finishing with a final dollop of cream. Drizzle the raspberry coulis around the edges and sprinkle the extra lavender flowers over the top. Serve at once.

Serves 4

blueberry and lavender pancake stack

date and pecan desserts with brandied toffee sauce

$^1/_3$ cup pecans, chopped

1 cup pitted dates, chopped

1 teaspoon pure vanilla extract

$^3/_4$ teaspoon baking soda

$^1/_3$ cup butter, softened

$^2/_3$ cup superfine sugar

2 eggs

1$^1/_2$ cups self-rising flour, sifted

brandied toffee sauce

1 cup soft brown sugar, lightly
   packed

1 cup whipping cream

$^1/_4$ cup butter, cubed

1 teaspoon pure vanilla extract

2–3 tablespoons brandy, to taste

whipping cream, to serve
   (optional)

Preheat the oven to 350°F.

Grease six 1-cup metal or ceramic molds and sprinkle the chopped pecans over the bottom. Put the molds on a cookie sheet.

In a large heatproof bowl, combine the chopped dates with $^2/_3$ cup boiling water. Stir in the vanilla and baking soda. Set aside to cool and to soften the dates.

In a medium bowl, beat the butter and sugar with electric beaters until thick and creamy, about 2 minutes. Add the eggs one at a time, beating well between each addition. Fold in the sifted flour with a metal spoon, then fold in the date mixture. Spoon the mixture into the prepared molds, filling them three-quarters full. Bake until firm to the touch and well risen, about 25 minutes.

For the toffee sauce, combine the sugar, cream, butter, and vanilla in a small saucepan. Stir over a low heat to dissolve the sugar, then bring to a boil. Simmer until slightly thickened, 10–15 minutes. Remove from the heat, cool a little, and then stir in brandy to taste.

Remove the desserts from the oven, set aside for 5 minutes. With the aid of a small, flat-bladed knife, turn them out onto serving plates. Pour the hot sauce over and serve with some cream if liked.

Notes: The desserts should be served hot, with the sauce a little absorbed into them. If not serving immediately after cooking, you can microwave the desserts and reheat the sauce. The desserts can be frozen for up to a month; before serving, thaw them, then microwave to reheat them. The sauce will keep refrigerated for a week.

Serves 6

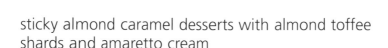

sticky almond caramel desserts with almond toffee shards and amaretto cream

almond toffee
3/4 cup superfine sugar
1/3 cup unblanched whole
    almonds, toasted

desserts
1/3 cup unsalted butter, softened
2/3 cup dark brown sugar
2 eggs
11/3 cups self-rising flour
3 tablespoons buttermilk
1 teaspoon pure vanilla extract
1/3 cup unblanched whole
    almonds, chopped

caramel sauce
1/3 cup dark brown sugar,
    firmly packed
11/2 tablespoons unsalted butter
2/3 cup whipping cream

Amaretto cream
1/3 cup heavy whipping cream
1 teaspoon Amaretto (almond
    liqueur)

For the almond toffee, slowly heat the sugar with 2 tablespoons water in a shallow saucepan until the sugar melts, stirring and brushing down the sides of the pan with water. Increase the heat to medium and simmer without stirring until it is a light golden color, about 3 minutes. Put a sheet of foil on a cookie sheet and sprinkle the almonds in a single layer in the middle. Remove the toffee from the heat, let the bubbles subside, then pour it over the nuts. Quickly tilt the sheet to coat evenly. Leave to harden.

For the desserts, grease six tall ³/₄-cup dariole molds. Line the bottom with a circle of parchment paper. Using electric beaters, beat the butter and sugar in a medium bowl until light and fluffy. Beat in the eggs one at a time. Gradually fold in the flour, then stir in the buttermilk and vanilla. Fold in the almonds. Divide among the prepared molds, filling them just over halfway. Level the tops. Cover each with a circle of parchment paper. Cut 6 squares of foil about 2 inches larger than the top of the molds and fold each square loosely over a mold, leaving a space underneath for the desserts to expand. Tie the foil onto the molds. Place a round wire rack in the bottom of a saucepan or use a large scrunched-up piece of foil, 10 inches diameter or just large enough to place the molds. Carefully pour cold water into the saucepan to come about 1¹/₂ inches up the sides of the molds. Cover the pan and bring to a boil over medium heat. Lower the heat and simmer for 30 minutes.

For the caramel sauce, stir the sugar and butter in a small saucepan over low heat until the butter melts. Add the cream and simmer for 5 minutes. For the Amaretto cream, mix the cream and Amaretto together well. To serve, remove the desserts from their molds and place onto serving plates, spoon over the caramel sauce, and drizzle the Amaretto cream around the bottom. Break the toffee into shards and put a couple in the top of each dessert. Serve at once.

Serves 6

sticky almond caramel desserts with
almond toffee shards and amaretto cream

hazelnut coffee cream cake

hazelnut topping
2 tablespoons butter, melted
2 tablespoons superfine sugar
2 tablespoons cane syrup or
    unsulfured molasses
1 cup hazelnuts, toasted and
    skinned (see note, page 41)

cake
3 eggs, separated
heaping $1/2$ cup superfine sugar
1 teaspoon pure vanilla extract
$2/3$ cup cornstarch

1 teaspoon baking powder
scant 1 cup hazelnuts, toasted,
    skinned, and ground

coffee cream
$2/3$ cup whipping cream
3 teaspoons confectioners' sugar
1 teaspoon instant coffee
    granules
1 tablespoon Tia Maria or other
    coffee liqueur

confectioners' sugar, to dust

Preheat the oven to 350°F. Grease a 9-inch round pan and line the bottom with parchment paper.

For the hazelnut topping, combine the melted butter, superfine sugar, and cane syrup in a small bowl. Coarsely chop half of the hazelnuts. Sprinkle the whole and chopped hazelnuts over the bottom of the prepared pan. Drizzle the butter mixture carefully over the nuts and spread evenly.

To make the cake, beat the egg whites to firm peaks with electric beaters in a small bowl, gradually adding the sugar. Beat for 3 minutes or until thick and glossy. Beat in the egg yolks one at a time, then the vanilla extract. Transfer the mixture to a larger bowl. Using a metal spoon, fold in the combined sifted cornstarch and baking powder alternately with the ground hazelnuts.

Carefully spoon the mixture into the prepared pan over the hazelnuts. Smooth the surface. Bake until well risen, firm, brown, and a skewer inserted into the center of the cake comes out clean, about 35 minutes. Leave in the pan for 10 minutes before turning onto a wire rack to cool completely. If any nuts have stuck to the parchment paper, return them to the top of the cake.

For the coffee cream, beat the cream and confectioners' sugar until thick. Dissolve the coffee granules in 1 teaspoon warm water. Beat the coffee and liqueur into the cream. To assemble, cut the cake in half horizontally. Spread the bottom half thickly with the cream and place the other half on top, with the hazelnuts facing up. Dust the top with confectioners' sugar.

Serves 8–10

baked rhubarb amaretto cream mille-feuilles

Amaretto cream

2 egg yolks

2 tablespoons superfine sugar

1 tablespoon all-purpose flour

3/4 cup milk

2 tablespoons Amaretto
(almond liqueur)

12 ounces rhubarb (about
2 1/2 medium stems rhubarb),
leaves removed, stems
washed, trimmed and cut
into 2-inch lengths (you will
need about 8 ounces after
trimming)

3 tablespoons superfine sugar

3 tablespoons white wine

2 sheets frozen butter puff pastry

1 egg

3 tablespoons whipping cream

confectioners' sugar,
to dust

For the Amaretto cream, beat the egg yolks, sugar, and flour until creamy in a small bowl using electric beaters. Put the milk in a small saucepan and bring slowly to a boil. Slowly pour into the Amaretto cream with the beaters running. Return the mixture to the saucepan and whisk constantly until the mixture boils and thickens. Remove from the heat and stir in the liqueur. Pour into a bowl, cover, and refrigerate until cold.

Preheat the oven to 350°F. Put the rhubarb pieces into a baking dish that holds them in one layer. Sprinkle with the sugar and wine, then bake until tender but still retaining their shape, about 20 minutes. Cool in the juices, then chill.

Increase the heat to 425°F. Line a large cookie sheet with parchment paper. Brush the pastry sheets with egg beaten with 2 teaspoons water. Cut each pastry sheet into 9 even squares. Arrange on the prepared sheet, well spaced. You may need to do this in two batches. Prick the pastry squares all over with a fork. Bake until golden and puffed, 10–12 minutes. Remove from the oven and trim away any edges that are stuck together, so that the pastry flakes are visible. Allow to cool.

Assemble the mille-feuilles just prior to serving. Beat the cream to soft peaks and gently fold into the Amaretto cream. Put each of 6 squares of pastry onto a serving plate and a spoonful of Amaretto cream onto the center of each. Cover with some of the rhubarb and a drizzle of juice. Put another square of pastry on top (there is no need to be too formal; the stacks can be slightly angled and free-form) and press down gently. Add another spoonful of cream and the remaining rhubarb and juice. Top with the final layer of pastry and dust liberally with confectioners' sugar.

Serves 6

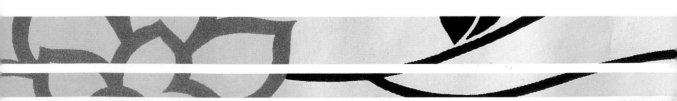

index

415